Vienna Opera 4 Apr 1999

set: opens w/ shadows creating
suggestion of prison (?)

peasants: pastoral feast ... creates
contrast w/ Don G's feast

set: touches of art nouveau in
design; otherwise lavish, 2-touches
lots of dark spots
3 maskers at ball — creates sense of
impending doom ... costumes
make them more powerful than
Don G.

Leporello — strongest applause from
audience

Opera
Guide

Don
Giovanni
Mozart

Ezio Pinza as Don Giovanni with Virgilio Lazzari as Leporello in the 1934 Salzburg production (Ida Cook Collection)

Preface

This series, published under the auspices of English National Opera, aims to prepare audiences to enjoy and evaluate opera performances. Each book contains the complete text, set out in the original language together with a current performing translation. The accompanying essays have been commissioned as general introductions to aspects of interest in each work. As many illustrations and musical examples as possible have been included because the sound and spectacle of opera are clearly central to any sympathetic appreciation of it. We hope that, as companions to the opera should be, they are well-informed, witty and attractive.

Nicholas John
Series Editor

18

Don Giovanni

Wolfgang Amadeus Mozart

Opera Guide Series Editor: Nicholas John

Published in association with
English National Opera

 John Calder · London
Riverrun Press · New York

First published in Great Britain, 1983, by
John Calder (Publishers) Ltd, 9-15 Neal Street,
London WC2H 9TU

and

First published in the U.S.A., 1983, by
Riverrun Press Inc., 1170 Broadway,
New York, NY 10001

Second Impression 1990

BRITISH LIBRARY CATALOGUING IN PUBLICATION DATA

Mozart, Wolfgang Amadeus
   Don Giovanni.—(Opera guides; 18)
   1. Mozart, Wolfgang Amadeus. Don Giovanni
   2. Opera—Librettos
   I. Title   II. John, Nicholas   III. Series
   782.1'1   ML50.M939

   ISBN 0-7145-3853-1

LIBRARY OF CONGRESS CATALOGING IN PUBLICATION DATA is available

English National Opera receives financial assistance from the Arts Council of Great Britain.

Typeset in Plantin by Maggie Spooner Typesetting, London NW5.

Printed in Great Britain by The Camelot Press, Southampton.

Contents

List of Illustrations

The 'Comic' Element in 'Don Giovanni'

Michael F. Robinson

If Mozart had had more freedom to compose whatever he liked, there is no doubt he would have written more operas than he did. His own letters make it clear he preferred composing operas to anything else. 'Don't forget my wish to write operas', he wrote to his father from Mannheim in February 1778, 'Italian, please, not German; serious, not comic.' Later, after he had settled in Vienna, he changed allegiance, imagining it was his duty to compose German rather than Italian opera. The company then at the Burgtheater in Vienna consisted of German-speaking actors and singers engaged by the Emperor to present plays and operas in the vernacular. It was for this company that Mozart composed *Die Entführung aus dem Serail* (*The Seraglio*) in 1782. That apart, few of the German operas at the Burgtheater were good enough to persuade the public wholeheartedly to support the venture. So in April 1783 the Emperor disbanded the troupe and replaced it with an Italian opera company — not a company intent upon performing *opera seria*, the genre of Italian opera that Mozart seems to have preferred, but *opera buffa*, since that was the genre more to the taste of the Viennese public as a whole. This explains why Mozart's two subsequent works for the Burgtheater, *Le Nozze di Figaro* (*The Marriage of Figaro*) (1786) and *Così fan tutte* (1790), were both Italian comic operas. The presence of the Italians in Vienna was also indirectly responsible for the creation of Mozart's other great Italian comic opera of that decade, *Don Giovanni*.

At the beginning of 1787 *The Marriage of Figaro* was given in Prague and Mozart travelled there from Vienna to see the production. Because the reception given the composer and his opera by Prague audiences was so favourable, the local impresario Bondini invited him to compose a new opera in time for the following autumn. The result was *Il dissoluto punito ossia il Don Giovanni*, first seen in Prague's Nationaltheater on October 29, 1787. It is important to realise that when Mozart and his librettist Lorenzo da Ponte selected the story of Don Giovanni for their new opera they did so believing it

'La ci darem la mano'
with Carlo Zuchelli
and Laure
Cinti-Damoreau
in Paris in the
1820s.

Henrietta Sontag as Donna Anna in Paris, 1826 (Royal Opera House Archives)

would form the basis of an opera much in the manner of *Figaro*. An opera completely different from *Figaro* would not have fitted Bondini's requirements. A modern observer, making a superficial comparison between *Figaro* and *Don Giovanni*, might however conclude that the two operas are wide apart. *Figaro*, for all that it makes serious comment on the society of Mozart's day, is yet obviously a comic opera with a happy ending. *Don Giovanni* has a generally graver tone. In this work the hero endangers the whole lifestyle of society through his actions; as chastisement he is dragged down to hell; the other characters, much relieved by his disappearance, end the opera with a warning to the audience that evil will not go unpunished. Hardly one's usual idea of a 'comic' subject! Yet Mozart and da Ponte called *Don Giovanni* a *dramma giocoso*, the same term they had used for *The Marriage of Figaro*. And they did so because both works had the technical features associated with Italian comic opera (whatever its designation: *dramma giocoso, opera buffa, commedia per musica*, etc.). These technical features had only a partial bearing on the amount of comedy or tragedy in the plot of an opera. So what were they?

All drama, according to Italian 18th-century theorists, had to instruct audiences to eschew evil and do good. To them the role of theatre was a didactic one. The only question was not whether but how drama should affect an audience for the better. In tragedy (and its operatic equivalent *opera seria*)

8

the public was supposed to be provoked to pity by the sight of the hero overcome by the forces of evil. Both the hero and those around him had in this type of drama to be high-class persons such as kings, princes, and important functionaries of their courts. Comedy (and *dramma giocoso/opera buffa*) was supposed to teach people how to avoid certain 'bourgeois' foibles like miserliness, credulity, uncouthness, charlatanism, by holding up these foibles to ridicule. Such traits being considered contemptible and undignified, they were associated with the lower and middle classes and these were the classes depicted in traditional staged comedy. By the late 18th century, however, librettists were adding a proportion of high-class characters to the *dramatis personae* of comic operas. They thus brought together on stage a wide spectrum of society, the servants, the bourgeoisie, the lower (if not, normally, the higher) orders of the nobility, to be deployed for effective dramatic and musical ends.

This wide variety of character types in comic opera led Italians to make a threefold classification of them, and everyone who attended the theatre in Mozart's day knew what they were. There were first of all the so-called 'serious' characters (*parti serie*), who displayed qualities like earnestness, courage, steadfastness, sensitive and passionate feelings concerning love and honour — such qualities were more likely to be assigned, though they were not in every case, to the higher classes than to the lower. There were then the 'comic' characters (*parti buffe*), usually from the lower classes, who displayed the opposite tendencies: inconstancy, cowardice, coarse feelings, deviousness and/or servility. Finally, for the reason that it was undesirable to split the cast into two completely contrasted serious and comic groups, librettists often included one or more *mezzi caratteri*, 'middle characters', who had either no facets of personality that identified them as serious or comic or else facets of both. This cast division also invited some differentiation between the musical languages of the characters, and there was a common belief in the 18th century (Mozart adhered to it) that, for example, a fast *parlando* was suitable for a comic character and, vice versa, roulades and vocalisations were suitable for a serious one. The differences in the characters' musical styles did not mean, however, that they could not sing together. Indeed an essential feature of any comic opera of the 1780s was the large ensemble for the majority of the characters at the end of each act (in the case of *The Marriage of Figaro* at the ends of Acts Two and Four). These finales, so characteristic of *opera buffa*, were not common in *opera seria* and so served as a technical feature that distinguished the one genre from the other.

Don Giovanni has all the aspects of a 'comic' opera that have been described. The three representatives of the lower classes, Leporello, Masetto, and Zerlina, are clearly 'comic'; Donna Anna and Donna Elvira are 'serious', and Don Ottavio, though more colourless than they, might well be classified as serious too. Don Giovanni, who has a chameleon-like quality of changing his manner to suit the society he is with (equally at home making advances to the lowly Zerlina as to Donna Anna), is a *mezzo carattere*. The Commendatore does not appear often enough to impress his character upon us as the others do, but probably he would be considered 'serious' if classification were required for him also. As for the music, Mozart makes his own brilliant differentiation of serious and comic personalities. Finally the work has many ensembles including the essential finales at the end of acts. Nothing more was required to give the work the ingredients of a 'comic' opera, according to the 18th-century understanding of that term, and Mozart and da Ponte might have been puzzled had they had any premonition of the future debates that were to take place over whether they thought their opera was comic or tragic.

'Vedrai carino' with Teresa Cahill and Robert Lloyd in John Copley's production at Covent Garden in 1973 (photo: Zoe Dominic)

A debate upon the actual amount of comedy and tragedy in *Don Giovanni* is, however, relevant in the context of a general survey of the development of comic opera. Whereas librettists 50 years earlier had concentrated on farce, by Mozart's time many were adopting a critical tone about society and were becoming concerned about issues like personal freedom and personal choice, the misuse of justice and the right of the ordinary man to be protected by the law. It was now not uncommon for opera to raise the issue of abuse of power by those with legal authority (for example, the Count in *Figaro*) or by armed force. As a result, many an operatic hero is constrained from marrying his sweetheart, and many a maiden is threatened with death or with a fate worse than death. In such circumstances what does the tone of an opera become? It becomes either sentimental, as hero and/or heroine and those close to them bewail their fate, or full of suspense, putting the audience on tenterhooks to see whether the right people will be saved. Although farce still has a role to play here, it becomes less evident as opera is made to serve a more serious purpose. The sudden popularity of Don Giovanni as a subject for opera in the 1770s is a symptom of this 'serious' trend within comic opera. Between 1776 and February 1787 there appeared no fewer than seven different Italian operas based on this particular story. Mozart's was thus the eighth one on the theme to appear in little more than a decade.

The story itself originated in a play by the early 17th-century Spanish playwright Tirso de Molina called *El burlador de Seville, y convidado de piedra*. In this play are already many of the ingredients of the story that were to be used time and time again in later versions: the hero who is an attractive and reckless seducer; the valet who occasionally protests at his master's actions but usually aids them; the father murdered by the hero while defending his daughter's honour; the hero's invitation to the statue of the murdered man to

10

Richard Van Allan as Don Giovanni and Malcolm King as Leporello in Anthony Besch's production for ENO, 1976 (photo: John Garner)

supper and the statue's acceptance; and finally the statue's revenge by dragging the hero to hell. When the play was brought to Italy, its theme was adopted by *commedia dell'arte* troupes as a basis for some of their improvised comedies. The theme was then also adopted by recognised playwrights in several countries. To take the best-known cases, Molière used it in his *Don Juan, ou le festin de pierre* (1665), Shadwell in his *The Libertine* (1676), and Goldoni in his *Don Giovanni Tenorio, ossia il dissoluto* (1736). Every playwright had to decide how much emphasis to put, on the one hand, on the figure of the Don himself and his reckless, immoral behaviour and, on the other, on the figure of the valet. The valet was, and is, potentially a humorous character because of the wide discrepancy between his pretensions and his performance. No man serving an apparent monster of depravity can be human and not remonstrate against his misdeeds, yet no man can still be valet and not do what he is told. Once committed to supporting Don Giovanni, the man then finds that a life of depravity is actually good fun but the excitement of it all goes to his head and he is in trouble. The occasions for broad comedy that the valet provides have persuaded many leading actors in the past to play his part rather than that of his master. Molière, for instance, acted the role of the servant Sganarelle, not that of Don Juan, in his own version of the story.

What role to give the valet was an equally important decision for the many operatic librettists who tackled the subject from the 1770s onwards. Leporello, in da Ponte's version, has many of the comic attributes traditionally associated with the part. He has scruples but his greed overcomes them (as when he accepts money from Don Giovanni); he is boastful (as when he recounts his master's exploits in the so-called 'catalogue aria' in Act One); he willingly acts his master's part (as when the two of them change clothes) and mismanages it; he lacks courage when it is tested (as when he hides under the table on the arrival of the statue in the Act Two finale). This clownish element in his character serves partly as a foil to Don Giovanni. Yet the more we observe the relationship between master and servant the more we realise that Mozart and da Ponte were not aiming to make one the opposite of the other. Don Giovanni and Leporello are in fact complementary. The two together provide the impulse for the action, and the other characters only come alive in so far as their feelings and deeds are reactions to Don Giovanni or Leporello or, more commonly, the pair of them.

If Leporello tries to be like Don Giovanni, Don Giovanni is not so unlike Leporello as to make an alliance between them implausible. Don Giovanni, let us reemphasise, is a *mezzo carattere*; that is, he has a comic as well as a serious side to his nature. He is not portrayed by Mozart or da Ponte as an out-and-out villain. Compared with the sins of some of his namesakes in earlier dramas, his seem mild. He is not even successful as seducer, and we are dependent upon Leporello's and Donna Elvira's word, and upon the traditional view of the man built up by other dramatists, for our belief that he has had his way with women before the curtain rises. During the opera itself, however, his attempts at seduction are all bungled. It seems clear from the music, witness especially the effervescent *'Fin ch'han dal vino'* ('Get them all drinking') in Act One, and his lighthearted serenade to Donna Elvira's maid in Act Two, that Mozart imagined his hero to possess a nature that was basically happy-go-lucky and carefree. The music does not accord with the image of a seducer single-mindedly resolved to carry his schemes through to their ultimate conclusion (a point to be borne in mind by anyone who imagines that Don Giovanni's character is all black). Might not part of the horror of Don Giovanni's end be due to the fact that we cannot imagine his misdeeds to merit quite so savage a fate?

Whether it is true or not that the 'comic' element in the character of Don Giovanni makes his downfall seem more 'tragic' than it would otherwise have been, there is truth in the more general proposition that happiness and humour are more effective on stage when used as a counterpoise to tears and sorrow than when used on their own. This is valid for all comedy, regardless of how it ends. What is interesting about the other 'comic' characters in the opera, Masetto and Zerlina, is that they are neither particularly humorous (as Leporello is) nor are they on Don Giovanni's and Leporello's side. By the end they have formed an alliance with the three serious characters against Don Giovanni, so that the party opposing him consists of people of all types. Zerlina is 'comic' in the sense that she is not afraid of a little coquetry with Don Giovanni when she first meets him, even in the presence of her fiancé Masetto. Masetto responds to her unfaithfulness by sulking and then planning to attack her seducer by brute force, neither reaction showing good breeding or the sort of dignity appropriate to a gentleman of high class. Once both have understood from bitter experience how the Don Giovanni/Leporello team has used and misused them, their next reaction is to find strength in each other's company and mend their quarrel. In the scene in Act Two in which Zerlina finds the much-battered Masetto on the ground and comforts his wounds and his injured pride, we have the sort of genuine pathos, the expressions of authentic tenderness, that are the real foil to Leporello's humour. Pathos in fact is the other side of any genuine comedy, and its appearance confirms the fact that Mozart's *Don Giovanni* is comic (*giocoso*) in essence as well as by definition.

Music and Action in 'Don Giovanni'

David Wyn Jones

From 1784 Mozart kept a catalogue of his music in which he recorded dates of completion together with musical incipits and a short description of every work. On October 28, 1787, the day before the *première* of *Don Giovanni*, the following details were noted: '*Il dissoluto punito* or *Don Giovanni*. *Opera buffa* in Two Acts. — Pieces of music. 24. Actors. Ladies. Teresa Saporiti, Bondini and Micelli. Gentlemen. Passi, Ponziani, Baglioni and Lolli.'

In terms of 'pieces of music' *Don Giovanni* is the shortest of the three operas to librettos by Lorenzo da Ponte, a compactness that mirrors the absence of the delight in the absurd that is an inimitable part of *The Marriage of Figaro* and *Così fan tutte*. There are, naturally, moments of relaxation in *Don Giovanni* and certainly the central figure's destiny is not pursued with the same relentlessness that affects Wagner's Senta in *The Flying Dutchman* or Berg's Wozzeck, but there is, nevertheless, an inevitability about the action that is not so much to do with the fate of one individual as with the comforting morality that misdemeanours will be punished. It is no accident that the words 'fate' and 'destiny' are never mentioned in the libretto; all the characters sing instead of justice and vengeance. Mozart's alternative title, *Il dissoluto punito* (The Debauchee Damned), is, therefore, a better indication of the central concern of the opera and, though the title *Don Giovanni* is more striking, it shifts the balance onto the individual in a manner which Mozart and da Ponte were careful to avoid.

Many commentators have pointed out that Don Giovanni is never seen to be successful in his adventures in the opera; his attempted seductions of Donna Anna, Zerlina and Donna Elvira's maid are all thwarted. Nor does he dominate the score in musical terms; he sings in twelve of the twenty-four numbers of the Prague version, three more than his servant Leporello, four more than Donna Anna and five more than Donna Elvira. With three arias he

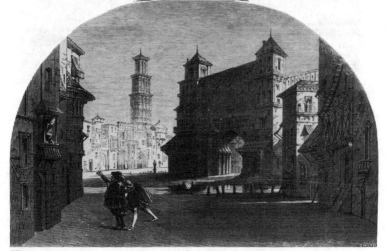

The serenade scene at Her Majesty's in 1846 (Theatre Museum)

Dino Borgioli as Don Ottavio (Stuart-Liff Collection)

has only one aria more than Leporello and Zerlina and, in the Viennese version, only one more than Donna Elvira and Don Ottavio too.

These statistics show that for Mozart the already dated conventions of 18th-century opera where the number of arias was allotted according to the standing of the singer and only secondarily according to the nature of the plot were irrelevant. More revealingly the nature of Don Giovanni's three arias shows a decided unwillingness to elaborate character and motivation. Don Giovanni does not have an extensive showpiece aria similar to Don Ottavio's '*Il mio tesoro*' ('On your affection relying') [35], Donna Elvira's '*Mi tradì*' ('He betrayed the love I gave him') [36] or Donna Anna's '*Or sai, chi l'onore*' ('You know now the traitor') [18]. His first aria occurs towards the end of Act One, the so-called champagne aria, '*Fin ch'han dal vino*' ('Get them all

Francesco D'Andrade as Don Giovanni and Lilli Lehmann as Donna Anna (Stuart-Liff Collection)

drinking') [20], a fleeting *buffo* aria, the sole dramatic point of which is to make the audience realise whose idea is the ball at the end of the Act. Don Giovanni's other arias occur in succession at the beginning of Act Two when the action is at its nadir. *'Deh vieni alla finestra'* ('Oh, look down from your window') [29] is headed *Canzonetta* and with its strophic structure (two verses) and mandolin accompaniment is a serenade of the most charming, but traditional, kind. In the following aria [30], Don Giovanni is still disguised as Leporello and, affecting the short *parlando* phrases of his servant, sends the villagers in search of himself who 'cannot be far from here' — again a stock comic situation that offers little insight into Giovanni's character. He is not allowed to speak for himself in an aria; the nearest thing to a statement of his philosophy of life occurs in Leporello's catalogue aria [9, 10] which, in its extended descriptions, is wickedly comic leaving all moral judgement to the listener.

To attempt to build a composite picture of Don Giovanni from his arias is therefore futile. Our image of the principal character is not formed so much from what he says of himself but from witnessing his interreaction with other characters in duets and ensembles, and noting the variety and strength of feeling his actions provoke in them.

At Covent Garden in the 19th century the opera was habitually performed in four acts, a division given respectability by Edward J. Dent who in his pioneering book *Mozart's Operas* (1913) conjectured that *Don Giovanni* was indeed first planned in four acts rather than two: Act One dealing with Don Giovanni and Donna Anna and concluding with her aria *'Or sai chi l'onore'* ('You know now the traitor') [18]; Act Two, Don Giovanni and Zerlina, ending where Act One now ends; Act Three, Don Giovanni and Donna Elvira, concluding with the Sextet [32]; and finally Act Four, Don Giovanni and the Commendatore. Though to a certain extent dramatically and musically plausible this division is only relevant to the final product as a simple *aide memoire* for the sequence of events; it tends to sectionalise the action in a way that focuses attention on Don Giovanni, and in that way undervalues the observations of those people who are not directly involved with Don Giovanni at any given stage in the continuing intrigue. Even Zerlina who might be regarded as a small cog in the dramatic action retains our interest and affection long after she has served as yet another episode in Don Giovanni's life. Her second aria, addressed to Masetto, *'Vedrai, carino'* ('My dearest lover') [31] is headed *'grazioso'* (with charm) and through a simple melodic line confined to no more than an octave's range creates a distinctive mood that none of the other characters can equal. Above all the main defect with a four-act view of *Don Giovanni* is that it breaks the symmetry of the action, particularly in the way the two acts move gradually towards their climaxes, two social scenes, a ball and a supper, both hosted by Don Giovanni. Making sure that the adventures of Don Giovanni are counterpoised and finally outweighed by the plotting of his adversaries is a continuing concern across the twenty-four musical numbers and one that is reinforced by the composer's deployment of keys and orchestral forces.

A register of keys used in the opera would show that D major is used more frequently than any other key; it is the key of the *Molto Allegro* of the overture [3, 4], Leporello's catalogue aria [9, 10], Donna Elvira's *'Ah fuggi il traditor'* [16], Donna Anna's *'Or sai chi l'onore'* [18], Don Giovanni's *Canzonetta* [29], a portion of the sextet, and the first and final portions of the second Act finale [39]. By dint of sheer emphasis the opera is in this key in the same way as the 'Prague' symphony is in D major and, though perhaps not all modern audiences respond to the brilliant sound of this key as Mozart's contemporaries did, its function as a base, point of reference and final home is a compelling one.

Only in the broadest sense can D major be associated with a mood, but its opposite mode, D minor, has strong atmospheric associations in the opera. In terms of number of appearances it occurs far less frequently: the introduction to the overture [1, 2], the duel in the first number, the duet between Donna Anna and Don Ottavio, *'Fuggi Crudele'* [6, 7] in the second number, Donna Elvira's address to the Maskers, *'Bisogna aver corragio'*, in the finale to Act One [24], and the lengthy scene with the Commendatore that leads to the death of Don Giovanni. Its appearances may be few but its dramatic impact is one of the most memorable and distinctive aspects of the score. Some of its effect derives from Mozart's shrewd avoidance of minor keys elsewhere but, more positively, there is the strong character of the D minor music itself.

D minor always elicited passionate music from Mozart, even in his earliest works in the key such as the overture to *La Betulia liberata* (K. 118) and a string quartet composed in 1773 (K. 173). An additional yearning melancholy is evinced in mature works like the string quartet (K. 421), the piano concerto (K. 466) and the unfinished requiem (K. 626). However, none of these has the same massive power associated with the key in *Don Giovanni*, especially in the introduction to the overture and the appearance of the Commendatore in the supper scene. Perhaps the only work to approach this sonority is the so-called 'Munich' *Kyrie* (K. 341), a single movement for chorus and large orchestra in a similarly measured *Andante* tempo. (The work is usually dated November 1780–March 1781; but Alan Tyson has recently suggested that it belongs, with several church music fragments, to the period December 1787–February 1789, that is to within sixteen months of the *première* of *Don Giovanni*.)

D major and D minor are the most significant keys in the opera and as such are an additional consideration to emotional atmosphere and vocal range

Jean-Baptiste Faure as Don Giovanni, a role he sang at Covent Garden in the 1870s (Theatre Museum)

Mattia Battistini as Don Giovanni, a role he first sang at Covent Garden in 1905 (Royal College of Music)

Geraint Evans as Leporello and Evelyn Lear as Donna Elvira at Covent Garden in the 1964/5 season (photo: Reg Wilson)

when keys are being chosen for other numbers. One of the most crucial choices was that for the finale of the first Act.

Don Giovanni is confronted by all his adversaries and though he eventually escapes, it is clear — abundantly so by the end of the finale — that the initiative in the action is slipping away from him. 'See the lightning flash of vengeance, angry Heaven parts asunder / And at last its wrath will thunder on your guilty head today!' sing the assembled company, except Leporello and Don Giovanni who prophetically assert 'But his (my) courage shall not fail him (me) / Though the powers of hell assail him (me)!' To have used D minor here would have pre-empted the force of the actual moment of vengeance and, moreover, to have ended the act in that key would be to deny the moral tone of the opera and would be as injurious to its message as the common 19th-century practice of ending the opera immediately after Don Giovanni's death. D major, as a major key would have been temperamentally suited to the situation but, as the home key, would run the risk of duplicating the second Act finale and, in general terms, over-emphasising D. The choice of C major avoids these pitfalls: it is only slightly less brilliant than D, has perhaps more aggression, and does not get in the way of the main keys.

Mozart's instrumentation complements his choice of key, not dogmatically so but in a way that weaves its own patterns. In the overture the audience is introduced to a full classical orchestra: two flutes, two oboes, two clarinets, two bassoons, two horns, two trumpets, timpani and strings. This full orchestra of strings, twelve wind and timpani is not heard again until the finale of Act One and, in Act Two, in the sextet and the finale where, for the scene leading to the death of Don Giovanni, it is reinforced by three trombones. For each of the remaining numbers Mozart varies the number of wind parts from none (in Donna Elvira's *'Ah fuggi il traditor'* [16]) to ten, and, as in the similarly varied instrumentation of the mature piano concertos, each aria gains much of its atmosphere from the particular combination of wind instruments added to the strings; there is for instance a tendency for the soft sounds of flutes and clarinets to be associated with Donna Elvira.

Equally distinctive and distinguished is Mozart's sure-footed sense of dramatic pacing. In many 18th-century operas the rate at which the drama is unfolded is so uniform that it becomes statuesque and therefore unreal; in Mozart the action is moulded into smaller and larger climactic peaks in a manner that holds attention and which the audience can perceive as credible. The seduction of 1003 women in Spain, and the appearance of a stone statue at supper, are in themselves unbelievable but what prevents them from seeming absurd in the theatre is the convincing presentation of motive, action and reaction. The music creates its own laws of reality that obliterate the unlikelihood of individual events.

Nowhere in the whole of Mozart's operas are these qualities put to a sterner test than in the opening of *Don Giovanni*. Within a quarter of an hour of curtain-up the audience is presented with a disgruntled servant, a failed seduction, a duel, a murder, a distraught daughter and an oath of vengeance.

The powerful overture diffuses its energies only in the last eleven bars, moving away from D major to the dominant of F major for the first scene. Leporello is pacing up and down in front of Donna Anna's house impatiently waiting for his master to appear; the pacing is indicated by the even tread of the music, the impatience by the brusque *forte* flourishes that conclude each phrase. The gait of the music as well as the key (F major) recalls another servant, Figaro, an intentional ruse on Mozart's part that immediately established a point of contact with the Prague audience who, in the composer's own words, 'talk of nothing but Figaro'. Like the beginning of the earlier opera

Gerald Davies as Don Ottavio and Victoria Sladen as Donna Anna in the 1949 Sadler's Wells production by Geoffrey Dunn (photo: Angus McBean © Harvard Theatre Collection)

that of *Don Giovanni* is lightweight, but a lot of information is imparted too. Leporello may be impatient, yet there is admiration for his master, shown in the clear desire to be a gentleman (Ex. A). The sympathy excited by this cameo portrait is, however, soon to be tested. Unlike the opening numbers of *The Marriage of Figaro* and *Così fan tutte*, Leporello's aria does not come to a formal ending followed by a recitative and another self-contained number; it could have done so quite easily with an orchestral flourish at bar 70 after the final statement of *'non mi voglio far sentir'* ('I must not get in their way'). Instead, by the simple device of a swift modulation from F major to B flat major emphasized by a rapid *crescendo*, the audience's attention is directed to another part of the stage where Don Giovanni is trying to escape from Donna Anna. This, the second event in the drama, is much more musically active. The pauses which allowed the audience to absorb Leporello's character disappear, there is more contrast in dynamics, the rhythms are more agitated and three people now sing rather than one. Mozart makes sure that Leporello's commentary is clearly heard — after all he is the only person the audience yet knows — and while Don Giovanni and Donna Anna argue and struggle in similarly shaped vocal lines, Leporello's vocal line contrasts with both (Ex. B).

The commotion is interrupted by the arrival of Donna Anna's father, the Commendatore, announced by another change in the music. The key moves away from B flat major to G minor, the rate of harmonic change is much slower, to suggest the imposing presence of the older man, and there is much use of dotted rhythms and unison. The actual tempo of the music has not altered from the time the curtain went up but by changing the amount of surface activity and the key Mozart has been able to intensify the drama gradually. Don Giovanni responds to the Commendatore's challenge to a duel, accepting the fight in the fateful key of D minor, which the overture has vividly implanted in the consciousness of the listener (Ex. C). The Commendatore is wounded, and only at that point does the tempo change, to a rather static *Andante*, allowing the pent-up tension to be released slowly while the Commendatore dies. The section, in F minor, never reaches a formal close, which might have sounded prosaic, but merges with the ensuing recitative.

Having shown the dramatic, unexpected incident that is to lead inevitably to the death of Don Giovanni, Mozart now has the problem of portraying the reaction that is to fuel the desire for revenge. To be credible the reaction has to come from a person with whom the audience can identify: to blurt it out in an ordinary recitative would be to forego the heightened sense of drama; a forceful aria along the lines of the later *'Ah fuggi il traditor'* would be more convincing if rather formal. Mozart's solution covers all dramatic exigencies. Donna Anna's immediate reaction is announced in *recitativo stromentato* (accompanied recitative), the unpatterned phrase structure allowing her to be convincingly distraught and encouraging Mozart to comment forcibly on individual words and phrases — *'sangue'* ('bleeding'), *'piaga'* ('wound'), *'Ei non respira più'* ('His heart has ceased to beat') etc.. It also allows Don Ottavio's personality to be communicated; from the start we are made aware that, though well-meaning, he is something of a broken reed. The ensuing formal duet in D minor [6, 7] confirms our impressions and shows that Donna Anna has gained sufficient composure to marshal her thoughts, the return to *recitativo stromentato* for the vital sentence *'Ah vendicar, se il puoi, giura quel sangue ognor!'* ('Swear to avenge my father,/Swear it by Heaven above!') emphasising both the forcefulness of the sentiment as well as its importance in the opera.

With this statement of intent the whole moral direction of the opera is

Marie McLaughlin and Ruggero Raimondi in 'La ci darem' at Covent Garden in 1981 (photo: Donald Southern)

clearly marked out. Up to this point Mozart has concentrated, in a masterfully controlled manner, on characterising the virulence of the action so that the subsequent long haul across two acts to the moment of vengeance is seen to be as just as it is inevitable. No other Mozart opera has quite the same shape to its dramatic contour. The graph begins at a high point and is followed by a long, steady climb to the end of Act Two with several lesser peaks and some carefully managed troughs on the way. The end of Act One is obviously a major climax but perhaps less obvious is the care with which Mozart restarts the process at the beginning of the second Act.

In 18th-century Italian opera it was the custom to begin the second act and later acts (if there were any) with *secco* recitative to ease the audience back into the action. Here, as in Act Two of *The Marriage of Figaro*, but for very different reasons, there is no preparatory recitative. Four brusque chords precede an argument between Don Giovanni and Leporello that is clearly an aftermath of the close escape at the end of Act One. The tension gradually decreases as Leporello is bought off, and the audience is prepared for the most leisurely sequence of numbers in the whole opera. The Trio [28], *Canzonetta* [29] and aria *'Metà di voi quà vadano'* ('Let half of you go over there') [30] may be leisurely but the forward impetus is still there, if only because of the unconventional beginning to the act. In the context of the dramatic pacing of the opera as a whole, these numbers provide momentary repose rather than complete respite before the pace of events quickens once more.

This intuitive feeling for the pacing and timing of musical events in what can be called the middle and large dimensions is complemented in Mozart's mature operas by a luxuriance of detail that reveals an inexhaustible imagination.

The duet, *'La ci darem la mano'* ('There will our vows be plighted') [14, 15] soon became the best known number in the opera — its popularity reflected, for instance, in Beethoven's set of variations for two oboes and cor anglais composed *circa* 1796 — a position which it has maintained to this day. Beyond being a pretty tune it has a richness of meaning and nuance that are easily missed when the duet is heard as a single number out of context.

The scene is prepared in the preceding recitative. Don Giovanni has set his eyes on Zerlina, a peasant girl who is engaged to marry Masetto. Initially Zerlina resists Don Giovanni's advances but by the end of the recitative she has virtually agreed to accompany him to his house; any reservations she may have are outweighed by the prospect that she, a peasant girl, is to be associated with the aristocratic Don Giovanni. The rate and nature of the conversation in the recitative approximates to normal speech. In the duet the conversational exchange is slower and involves a good deal of repetition, allowing the resonances of the situation to be fully explored in a manner which the more literal recitative, or indeed normal speech, could never emulate.

Don Giovanni was composed in the wake of the successful performances of *The Marriage of Figaro* in Prague and there are points of similarity which the first night audience would have appreciated. These include certain parallels in the nature of the plot and in the characterization topped, in the finale to Act

'La ci darem la mano' with Maurice Renaud and Bessie Abott (Stuart-Liff Collection)

23

Gabriel Bacquier as Don Giovanni and Wladimiro Ganzarolli as Leporello at Covent Garden in 1969 (photo: Donald Southern)

Two, by an actual quotation from the earlier opera. Cultivating the good humour of his audience is always a prime consideration of Mozart in his operas and in *Don Giovanni* this is at its most audacious in the ball scene in the finale of Act One. Dancing to the accompaniment of a stage band is common enough in operas but Mozart's dance sequence has an enthralling quality that does not diminish with repeated hearings.

Don Ottavio and Donna Anna pace a courtly minuet to the accompaniment of a stage band [25]. Towards the end of the minuet a second stage band is heard tuning up with all the twitching mannerisms that string players employ to this day. This second stage band then plays a *Contredanze* in 2/4 against the continuing 3/4 of the minuet. During these two dances a third stage orchestra is heard tuning up; they proceed to play a *Deutscher* (a fast waltz) in 3/8, danced by Leporello and Masetto. Therefore, at the end of the sequence there are three stage bands playing three different dances in three different metres (Ex. D). Meanwhile, in the foreground, all the participants exchange views on the dramatic situation. Though no-one should underestimate the difficulties for the performers of keeping the music synchronized, but rhythmically distinct, in terms of counterpoint the actual feat of composing three different dances that combine is not as stunning as the contrapuntal intricacies of the finales of the G major quartet (K. 387) or the 'Jupiter' symphony (K. 551). It is not Mozart the skilled contrapuntist at the service of his art who is on display here, but Mozart the showman watching with increasing glee the reaction of his audience as each new dance appears.

There is a close precedent for this bold plan in Mozart's *oeuvre* which suggests that he may have been recalling an actual event. In December 1776–January 1777 at Salzburg Mozart composed a *Notturno* (K. 286) for four orchestras of strings plus two horns each. Though the circumstances of the performance are not known it can be assumed that the orchestras were widely separated. Orchestras two, three and four provide a triple echo of the music of the first orchestra and at other times the music is shared. In the last of the three movements, a minuet, Mozart cannot resist the temptation of duplicating

John Brecknock as Don Ottavio and Rita Hunter as Donna Anna in the 1976 ENO production (photo: John Garner)

what were probably very resonant acoustics and brings in the four orchestras in an overlapping fashion. The result, as in *Don Giovanni*, is not dissonant, just pleasantly confusing.

The exhilarating joy which results from witnessing such events in a live theatre (something which can never be captured on disc or on film), together with those highly developed aspects of Mozart's craft, dramatic pacing and characterisation, are qualities most brilliantly and extensively displayed in the finales to acts. All the da Ponte operas contain so-called chain finales, a series of musical sections at the end of an act played without the interruption of recitative for upwards of twenty minutes, the action and the music inter-reacting to create climax and denouement. While Mozart cannot be credited with the invention of the chain finale his use of it raised 18th-century opera to a height of dramatic realism that was not to be equalled for several decades.

It is in these continuous stretches of music that the audience becomes most aware of Mozart's ability to alter perspective from one moment to the next. In comparison with the aural perspective Mozart creates, the visual perspective of his operas in the theatre is of little consequence to their impact. One moment the music will be focused on the emotions of a single person, the next commenting in a detached manner on the general scene, the next directing the listener's attention to a particular event. In modern terms Mozart's music operates like a television or film camera with a full range of shots from wide-angle through zoom lens to close-up.

The Act Two finale opens with a 'wide-angle shot'. Although the music as Don Giovanni sits down to supper is light-hearted [39], the use of the full orchestra (minus trombones) in D major indicates that the opera is building up to its final climax. The listener's attention is drawn inwards when the stage band's *Harmoniemusik* begins. Leporello and Don Giovanni are treated to extracts from Martin y Soler's *Una cosa rara*, Sarti's *Fra i due litiganti il terzo gode* and Mozart's *Figaro*, the last a final gesture to the appreciative Prague audience and one that Leporello greets with the words 'That tune I know too well'. Members of the Prague audience who could also recall the words of *'Non più*

25

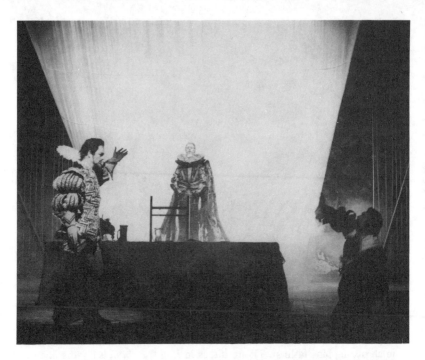

Peter Glossop as Don Giovanni, Geraint Evans as Leporello and Gwynne Howell as the
Commendatore in John Copley's 1973 Covent Garden production (photo: Zoe Dominic)

Ruggero Raimondi engulfed by hell-fire in Joseph Losey's film (photo: Artificial Eye)

Ruggero Raimondi as Don Giovanni and Gwynne Howell as the Commendatore in Peter Wood's production at Covent Garden in 1981, designed by William Dudley (photo: Donald Southern)

The Commendatore's entrance in Anthony Besch's ENO production, designed by John Stoddart (photo: John Garner)

andrai' would have appreciated the irony of the choice: 'No more will you go, amorous butterfly,/Night and day wandering round/Disturbing the repose of pretty women . . .'

With a sudden change of tempo to *Allegro assai* and of pulse to one-in-bar, attention is switched to the unexpected arrival of Donna Elvira who, rather like Fiordiligi in *Così fan tutte*, often sings in an indignant, high-flown manner that Mozart's contemporaries would have associated with an *opera seria* heroine. Here Elvira attempts to persuade Don Giovanni to change his way of living [40]. He refuses. She leaves the stage only to be confronted, as the chromatic writing and *sforzando* accents inform us, by the moving statue of the Commendatore. Leporello is sent to investigate, his subsequent report in the new faster tempo of *Molto Allegro* being both funny and frightening. Don Giovanni opens the door to the Commendatore and a savage diminished seventh chord announces the appearance of the stone guest and the beginning of the scene which, even by Mozart's standards, is one of the most remarkable in all his operas.

It hardly seems credible that a few minutes earlier the audience were casual onlookers at a pleasant supper scene; now they are closely caught up in the horror of a drama generated by music that Bernard Shaw described as 'beyond comparison the most wonderful of the wonders of dramatic music'*. The key is D minor, the music a vast extension of that heard in the introduction to the overture. Three trombones, always in 18th-century operas associated with the supernatural (Mozart himself had used them to accompany the utterances of the oracle in *Idomeneo*), add depth and weight to the sound; the harmonic progressions are sometimes of the most angular kind and emphatic cadences are few; dynamics are contrasted with Beethovenian power, in particular, the *crescendo* passages that lead to a sudden *piano*; and the orchestral writing, especially when it is supplemented by a unison male chorus, has a cut and thrust prophetic of Verdi.

The return to normality and the eventual pointing of the moral is as controlled as the earlier transition had been inevitable. In a bright, brisk G major the assembled company learns of Don Giovanni's fate from Leporello [42]. At this point no new information is being imparted but, as well as taking an interest in the reactions of the different individuals, the audience is able to recover some composure after the drama of the previous section. To prepare for the final *Presto* and to satisfy our curiosity concerning the future of the individual characters Mozart includes an expansive *Larghetto* in which all the participants announce their intentions; Donna Anna asks Don Ottavio for a year to recover before considering marriage, Donna Elvira is to enter a convent, Zerlina and Masetto cannot look further forward than their next meal together, and Leporello is to find a new and better master. All this is made perfectly intelligible by the slow tempo and adds a human touch to the forthcoming moral pronouncement which otherwise might have seemed pompous.

The *Presto* returns the audience to a final long-distance perspective while the moral is announced 'Sinners end as they begin./All who scorn the life eternal/Their eternal death shall win!'/It begins as a three-part fugato on Ex. E. Over a hundred years later Verdi was to end his opera *Falstaff* with a fully-fledged fugue on the words *'Tutto nel mondo e burla'* ('Everything in the world is a joke'). The alternation of *forte* and *piano* and the retreat into *piano* two-part writing before the final *forte* suggest that similar sentiments were not far from Mozart's mind.

* In a review of a Covent Garden performance in *The World* (May 13, 1891); *Music in London 1890–94* (London, Constable & Co. Ltd. 1932).

Musical Examples

Ex. A   LEPORELLO

Molto allegro

Violin 1

fp   *f*

I   was   made for wealth and   lei — sure

Ex. B   DONNA ANNA, DON GIOVANNI, LEPORELLO

Molto allegro

A. Like a   wild   a — veng — ing   fu — ry,   I'll pur-

G. If I   can't es — cape   this

L. the   end.   How   she's

sue   you   to   the   end.   Like a   wild   a-(venging fury)

fu — ry,   She will bring a — bout   my   end.

how — ling,   Oh   what   an   up — roar!

Ex. C   DON GIOVANNI

Molto allegro

If   you're   de — ter — mined   then   die   your   way!

Ex. D

Deutscher

Orch. III

Contredanze

Orch. II

Menuetto

Orch. I

29

Ex. E   DONNA ANNA, DONNA ELVIRA

Presto

Sin – ners   end   as   they   be – gin,   As
they   be – gin,   Sin – ners   end!

The cemetery scene at Covent Garden in 1973, designed by Stefanos Lazaridis. (photo: Stuart Robinson)

Lorenzo da Ponte

Christopher Raeburn

It was said that originally he was a Jew — turned Christian — dubbed himself an Abbé — and became a great dramatic writer ... He had a remarkably awkward gait, a habit of throwing himself (as he thought) into a graceful attitude, by putting his stick behind his back, and leaning on it; he had also a very peculiar, rather dandyish, way of dressing; for, in sooth, the Abbé stood mighty well with himself, and had the character of a consummate coxcomb; he had also a strong lisp and broad Venetian dialect.*

This description of da Ponte appears in the *Reminiscences* of Michael Kelly, the tenor, who doubled the roles of Don Basilio and Don Curzio in the original production of *The Marriage of Figaro*. But da Ponte had a long struggle before becoming a familiar personality in the theatrical life of Vienna, and achieving immortality as Mozart's librettist.

He was born Emmanuele Conegliano on March 10, 1749, the son of a Jewish tanner and leather dealer, in Ceneda near Venice. In 1763 his father became a Christian in order to remarry. The family also converted, and following custom, the Coneglianos adopted the surname of the Bishop of Ceneda, Lorenzo da Ponte, with the eldest son, Emmanuele, being baptised Lorenzo.

Up to this time he had had no schooling; he was known as *'lo spirito ignorante'* ('the witty ignoramus') and he grew up speaking Hebrew and Venetian. But after rummaging in an attic he found the works of Metastasio (1698–1782), the Italian poet who had held the Imperial post of Caesarean Poet since 1727. In all he wrote 27 librettos establishing and becoming the backbone of the *opera seria* tradition, in which the unities of the classical French drama were imposed on the Italian libretto; they proved to be one of the more significant discoveries of da Ponte's life. These librettos became the cornerstone of his literary background, and encouraged him to embark on a more formal education. Lorenzo and his brother Girolamo entered the seminary at Ceneda under the patronage of the Bishop, where they remained for five years. The object of the seminary was to prepare its pupils for the priesthood. As da Ponte recounted in his *Memoirs*, 'when I was seventeen, although I was able to compose a long oration and perhaps fifty not inelegant verses in Latin in half a day, I could not write a letter of a few lines in my own language without making a dozen mistakes.' But the young Abbate Cagliari introduced him to the great poets, inspiring in him a passion for Italian literature which he was to retain and pass on to his pupils throughout his life.

When he was nineteen da Ponte's studies were interrupted by a long illness, and in July 1768 his patron died leaving not only Lorenzo but his family in poverty. In the following year he was offered a teaching post at the seminary at nearby Portogruaro and in November 1770 he took holy orders, which probably assisted his appointment as Vice Rector there in April 1772. A year later he visited Venice, where he found the way of life irresistible; as the

* This passage comes from Michael Kelly's recollection of his own performances as the Poet in da Ponte's *Demogorgone ossia il filosofo confuso* (with music by Righini) given on July 12, 1786, in which he imitated da Ponte's mannerisms.

In the 19th century, Zerlina was the preferred role of many sopranos: Emma Albertrazzi, 1837 (left); and Fanny Persiani, 1838 (right). (Royal College of Music)

Venetians put it, 'A little Mass in the morning, a little gamble in the afternoon, and a little lady in the evening'. It was the little lady who proved to be da Ponte's undoing. He fell in love with Angiola Tiepolo, a member of one of the oldest patrician families. His adventures became successively more romantic and fantastic but he left in 1774 disillusioned and penniless to take up the appointment of Professor of Rhetoric at the seminary in Treviso. He was sufficiently brilliant intellectually to upset the establishment with his radical ideas which he aired more publicly than was wise. In 1776 he chose as the theme for the poems to be recited at the annual *Accademia*, 'Whether man is happier in an organised society or in a simple state of nature'. This was regarded as highly subversive, and he was forbidden to hold any further teaching post in the Venetian Republic, though he continued to live in Venice for the next three years. But in 1779 he was formally banished from the city for fifteen years on account of his affair with Angioletta Bellaudi, who was already married.

Da Ponte was by now exceptionally well-read and enjoyed a certain social success as an extemporary poet. Through his patron, the very wealthy Bernardo Memmo, he moved in the heart of the artistic and literary set. Venice was a focus of operatic activity in a period when Italian opera, both serious and comic, was fashionable in every court in Europe and at St Petersburg. Among the operas given at one or other of the Venetian opera houses in 1776 were premières of works by Anfossi, Bertoni, Sarti (his first success *Le Gelosie villane*, based on a play by Goldoni) and Bortnyansky; in 1777 a version of the Don Giovanni story, Callegari's *Il Convitata di Pietra*, was given during carnival; in 1778, there were first performances of operas by Traetta, Sarti and Salieri. This last, *La Scuola de' Gelosi*, had a text by the Court poet of Dresden, Caterino Mazzolà who, much later, was to adapt Metastasio's 1734 libretto of *La Clemenza di Tito* for Mozart. Another of da Ponte's acquaintances from these years was Giacomo Casanova, who maintained an erratic friendship with him and who may indeed have assisted

Adelina Patti made her debut as Zerlina at Covent Garden in 1861 (Theatre Museum)

Zarè Thalberg who first sang at Covent Garden in 1875 (Theatre Museum)

in retouching the libretto of *Don Giovanni*. He has left this description of the poet:

> an extraordinary man . . . known as a rogue of moderate wit, with great talents for being a man of letters and sufficient physical attractions to be loved . . . an original in every sense.

When he left Venice, da Ponte took refuge in Gorizia on the Austrian side of the Venetian border and produced some casual work for the local theatre. He received a letter purporting to be from Mazzolà offering him work in Dresden, and though the letter was a forgery, Mazzolà was generous enough to allow him to assist as a translator and adaptor. This invaluable experience of working in the theatre had a great influence on da Ponte. It was clear that this position could not last, however, and the rumour that the Emperor Joseph II might found an Italian Opera Company in Vienna led him, with many other librettists, composers and singers, to try his luck there.

One of the things he did on his arrival in Vienna was to present himself to the elderly Metastasio, who received him with approval, but when he died, in April 1782, his title (and income) of Caesarean Poet lapsed. Da Ponte, whose talents as a librettist were still untried, nevertheless became established in Viennese society because of his association with Salieri. His influence with Count Rosenberg, the Emperor's Chamberlain and Head of all Court Theatres, obtained for da Ponte the appointment of Poet to the Imperial Theatres at a salary of 1200 florins a year. He also commissioned a libretto for his projected opera, *Il ricco d'un giorno*. Unfortunately this work, first performed in December 1784, had been preceded in August by Paisiello's singularly successful *Il re Teodoro in Venezia*. The text for this *dramma eroicomico*, was the first libretto of the Abbé Giambattista Casti, who had begun writing for the theatre late in his career as a poet and satirist (he was sixty-two). It was drawn from a chapter in Voltaire's *Candide* which in turn was based on a historical episode when a German baron was adopted as King of Corsica (in 1736). He was expelled and travelled around Europe before he died in London; in the opera he reflects on his unfortunate fate and the collapse of his plans. The highly original libretto featured a number of unusual characters — a dispossessed Pasha for instance — and the title role was drawn with skilful sympathy. When Salieri's opera failed therefore, the composer hastily dropped da Ponte in favour of Casti. Their collaboration resulted in a work of a very different type: *La Grotta di Trofonio*, a comedy of magic and stage machines, which was also a huge success.

Vienna has always thrived on factions and intrigue; rivalries developed in the operatic world, helped in no small way by the singers themselves. Salieri's attachment to Catarina Cavalieri and da Ponte's own later affair with Ferraresi del Bene, two formidable prima donnas, contributed towards partisan behaviour and judgements. Casti was da Ponte's greatest rival since they worked in exactly the same field. The relationship between librettists in general was of a friend-foe nature, as was that between rival composers. Their mutual interests provided a background for daily intercourse and, while their material interests remained in common, a satisfactory social relationship prevailed. By contrast when they worked in competition the rivalry became vicious, and da Ponte was a master of intrigue and invective. He and Casti maintained this sort of ambiguous relationship during the years they coincided in Vienna, until they each at different times found themselves obliged to leave. In 1784 Casti had written his *Poema tartaro*, a satire on Catherine the Great and Russia, where he had spent many years. At the time it caused amusement in Vienna, but in 1786, when Austria was seeking a Russian alliance, Casti was advised, with financial help from the Emperor, to take an extended holiday.

After being abandoned by Salieri, da Ponte placed his hopes on Martin y Soler, a Spanish composer who had recently come to Vienna from Madrid, where he had written *zarzuelas* and *opere buffe*. Their chosen subject was a popular Goldoni text, *Il burbero di buon cuore*, and it turned out to be the composer's first great success when given in January 1786. In the following month Salieri and Casti produced a small masterpiece, *Prima la musica, e poi le parole* (*First the music, then the words*), a witty one act opera with topical allusions discussing the relative importance of the words and music in opera.

The piece was presented in a double-bill by command of the Emperor at Schönbrunn, with *Der Schauspieldirecktor*, a German spoken satire on contemporary theatre by Gottlieb Stephanie, and superb incidental music by Mozart. That was, however, less successful than the Italian opera and both Mozart and da Ponte were in need of a work to assure themselves of the favour of the Viennese public. Their turn of fortune came with the proposal by Mozart to adapt Beaumarchais's *Le Mariage de Figaro*. The composer and librettist had met socially in 1783. Although it has been surmised that da Ponte wrote the libretto for *Lo sposo deluso*, an unfinished opera for which Mozart composed five numbers, and he may also have translated the Latin text of Mozart's oratorio *Davidde Penitente* into Italian, their great collaboration started with *The Marriage of Figaro*.

It is unlikely that they were personal friends. Their Austrian and Venetian backgrounds did not have so much in common, and whereas da Ponte was basically a cynical opportunist, Mozart was a far more profound artist beneath his humorous exterior. But professionally their gifts as librettist and composer were ideally complementary.

Mozart had stressed to his father the importance of the collaboration between poet and musician: 'the best thing of all is when a good composer, who understands the stage and is talented enough to make sound suggestions,

Ryland Davies as Don Ottavio at Covent Garden (photo: Donald Southern)   *Tito Gobbi as Don Giovanni at Covent Garden (photo: Reg Wilson)*

meets an able poet.' We know from his letters that in 1780 Mozart had made considerable changes in Varesco's libretto of *Idomeneo* so that he was able to compose music which led from the set numbers into the recitatives, or from one number to another without a break. Certain radical differences between Bretzner's text for André's opera, *Belmonte und Constanze* (1781), Stephanie's source for Mozart's *Die Entführung aus dem Serail* (*The Seraglio*, 1782) and the final version, indicate that Mozart took a significant part in the adaptation of that text as well. It is of importance in any study of Mozart's librettos to appreciate that *The Seraglio, Figaro* and *Don Giovanni* were all adaptations of stage works. Da Ponte had considerable experience in adapting, either by translating existing works or improving them dramatically, and in tailoring pieces to please the authorities and provide opportunities for the singers. He had furthermore that stock-in-trade of great lyric writers: the facility for producing apt verse with neat allusions and a point. But the two great innovations of Mozart and da Ponte, first in *Figaro* and later in *Don Giovanni*, were the recitatives which lifted opera from its artificiality into the world of contemporary theatre, and the extended finales, which introduced a form of orchestrated recitative into the ensembles. While *Figaro* transcended the 'number' opera, the innovation was prompted by the nature of the play, which was both modern, and a comedy, not a farce. Not all da Ponte's work was by any means of this calibre; both *Figaro* and *Don Giovanni* owed much to his source material and to Mozart's unparalleled flair for transforming stage drama into opera.

After *Figaro* da Ponte wrote the libretto for Stephen Storace's *Gli Equivoci*, based on *The Comedy of Errors*, and for Martin y Soler's *Una cosa rara*, based on a story by another Spaniard, Luis Velez de Guevara, which had an immense success. He then received approaches for further work from Martin, Mozart and Salieri. As he put it in his *Memoirs*, 'I wondered whether it might not be possible to satisfy them all, and to write three operas at one and the same time'. Salieri required an Italian version of his own opera *Tarare*, which with a French text by Beaumarchais, in five acts and a prologue, had been enormously popular in Paris in 1787. This commission may have post-dated the other two by some months. Da Ponte suggested the allegory of *L'Arbore di Diana* for Martin, and the *Don Juan* story for Mozart to fulfil an operatic commission for Prague. In reply to the Emperor's doubts about attempting all three works at once, he replied: 'I shall write in the evenings for Mozart, imagining I am reading the *Inferno*; in the mornings I shall work for Martin and pretend I am studying Petrarch; my afternoons will be for Salieri. He is my Tasso!' After 63 days the first two works were complete, and *Tarare*, renamed *Axur, rè d'Ormus*, was well on its way.

Don Giovanni both as a play and comic opera was well known. Apart from the treatments by Molière and Goldoni, both certainly known to da Ponte, there were any number of recent reworkings of the theme. Gazzaniga had written a one act version to a libretto by Giovanni Bertati, which was produced in Venice in February 1787*. It served as a rough basis for da Ponte and Mozart. Don Giovanni and the Commendatore remain much the same. Donna Elvira is Don Giovanni's fiancée in the earlier version, and Donna Ximena his abandoned mistress; da Ponte dispensed with Donna Ximena and combined the two characters. Maturina and Biagio are the later Zerlina and Masetto. Donna Anna plays a less important role in the Bertati, so the roles of Donna Anna and Maturina could be doubled. Da Ponte gives Ottavio more to do, but reduces him from 'Duca' to being a mere 'Don'. Bertati gives Don Giovanni, two servants, Pasquariello and Lanterna, the former being a *servo confidente*, who not only accompanies his master on his exploits but also eats with him at table. Da Ponte's Leporello is socially in between Pasquariello and Lanterna, since he accompanies Don Giovanni on his adventures, although he serves him at table without joining him.

Both versions approximate up to the death of the Commendatore, and Elvira's entrance. Pasquariello has a Catalogue Aria from which da Ponte drew liberally. Don Giovanni seduces Ximena and Maturina, and Biagio is beaten up. All three ladies have been promised marriage and each expects to be preferred. The scene changes to the cemetery where the Duca Ottavio is instructing the stonemason to inscribe a curse. Don Giovanni's arrival there is roughly the same in both versions, but in Bertati the Statue's only words, *'Ci venirò'* ('I will come'), are less effective than da Ponte's succinct *'Sì'*. The two supper scenes differ in particular. Bertati brings in Donna Elvira before a knockabout scene between Don Giovanni and his servants. She urges him to repent and leaves after a final recitative and aria. Bertati gives the Don a song of praise for Venice, da Ponte a passage glorifying women. There are situations such as Pasquariello talking with his mouth full, and a band of house musicians, on which da Ponte was later to elaborate. Bertati included a *Brindisi* Trio, omitted in the later version, which may have inspired Don Giovanni's *'Fin ch'han dal vino'* ('Get them all drinking'). Da Ponte followed his source fairly closely from the entrance of the Statue to Don Giovanni's final downfall to hell. Both convention and Bertati's *scena ultima* served to suggest to da Ponte that his surviving characters should end the opera on a happy note, but in the earlier version, after formally condemning Don Giovanni, they join in a *'commedia dell'arte' buffo* finale imitating musical instruments, which would have been completely unsuitable in the later one. All Mozart's and da Ponte's characters, excepting possibly Donna Anna and Don Ottavio, are great creations and far transcend their counterparts in the Bertati.

* When da Ponte produced it in London in 1794, with a mixture of his own libretto and Bertati's, and additional music by other composers, it is probable that Mozart's Catalogue Aria was included — the first time it was heard in London. The whole of Mozart's opera was not performed there until 1817.

Da Ponte reminisced that Mozart wanted to make *Don Giovanni* a serious opera, and da Ponte prevailed upon him to make it a comedy. A hint of their compromise comes in titling the opera *dramma giocoso*. The successful juxtaposition of the serious element with the murder of the Commendatore and Donna Anna's revenge, and the humorous philosophies of Don Giovanni and Leporello, sophisticated and earthy respectively, give the work its unique quality. The subtlest borderline comes in the scenes between Don Giovanni, Leporello and Donna Elvira, where Elvira should never be overplayed and comedy descend to farce. Of the three 'serious' characters, Donna Anna, Don Ottavio and Donna Elvira, the latter is the most interesting by virtue of the way she reacts to the variety of situations in which da Ponte places her. No doubt da Ponte had personal experience to draw upon from the women he had left in the lurch.

Da Ponte went to Prague 'in order to direct the actors' taking part in *Don Giovanni*, but he was recalled to assist the final rehearsals of Salieri's *Axur* in Vienna. The first performance on *Don Giovanni* took place in Prague on October 29, 1787 to great acclaim. For its Vienna revival on May 7, 1788 Mozart and da Ponte composed a further aria for Donna Elvira, a duet for Leporello and Zerlina, and a substitute aria for Don Ottavio. The opera was only moderately well received.

At the end of the 1788 season in Vienna, the Emperor decided to close the Opera because of financial difficulties caused largely by the war. Da Ponte evolved a scheme to save it on a subscription basis which would make it self-supporting. Though there was much opposition on personal grounds from the theatrical administration, the Emperor agreed to the plan and doubled da Ponte's salary. Da Ponte had at last realised his dream of becoming poet-manager, the power behind the scenes.

His last collaboration with Mozart, *Così fan tutte*, was written in 1789 and first performed on January 26, 1790. In the 19th century it was thought to be immoral, but the pendulum has now swung so that some regard it as da Ponte's finest libretto, with its elegant diction, its cleverly devised symmetrical structure, and its opportunities for raising serious human issues within its artificial framework. Although the opera is couched in a stylised idiom, the comedy of manners emerges as true to life, and the sisters, if played seriously and without exaggeration, are both impressive and very funny. Furthermore Ferrando is a tenor hero (as opposed to a character tenor) with a sense of humour. *Così* provided Mozart with the opportunity of expressing the subtlest human emotions, and it resulted in the most sophisticated of all their joint works.

Da Ponte's position in Vienna was to be short-lived, since his affair with the soprano Ferraresi del Bene (the original Fiordiligi) gave his enemies ample ammunition to attack him, and he had few friends there anyway. In 1791 he was banished and had to give up his position as Poet to the Imperial Theatres. His successor in 1792 was not Casti as had been expected, but Bertati. When da Ponte called upon him, he was coldly received, but he noted that Bertati was not finding his position easy, and that he was surrounded by rhyming dictionaries.

Da Ponte took flight to Trieste and there met the daughter of an English merchant, Nancy Grahl, twenty years his junior and possibly Jewish. He married her and left with the idea of settling in Paris; when passing through Prague, however, he met Casanova again, who recommended that he should go to London, though he cautioned him: 'When you are in London, never set foot inside the Italian café and never sign your name to a bill'.

In London he obtained the post of Poet to the Italian Opera, and became the

The arrival of the maskers at Don Giovanni's palace from Joseph Losey's film (photo: Artificial Eye)

accredited representative of William Taylor, the Manager of the King's Theatre in the Haymarket. In 1797 he was sent to Italy to engage singers and, on his return to London, he had every reason to heed Casanova's warning since he found himself legally responsible for Taylor's debts. Although his problems were temporarily relieved by opening an Italian bookshop in London, in 1805 he fled his creditors and left with his wife and young family to join her relatives in New York. He started up as a grocer, but found more suitable occupation as a teacher of Italian. In time he became revered as the father of Italian Studies in America.

His last great moment of glory was the visit of Manuel Garcia and his Spanish operatic company to New York. In a season which included six Rossini operas, on May 23, 1826, Garcia presented at da Ponte's suggestion 'his' *Don Giovanni*. Garcia took the name role and Zerlina was sung by his eighteen-year-old daughter, Maria, who was shortly to become world-famous as Maria Malibran.

In 1823 da Ponte had started publishing his *Memoirs* which, though fanciful, give a vivid picture of his life and personality. He had always hoped for the foundation of a permanent Italian opera in New York, and was instrumental in bringing over an Italian Company in 1832 which, although well subscribed, had an unsuccessful season. Nevertheless, at great expense, a new Opera House was built in the following year, largely due to da Ponte's influence; but it was soon realised that opera was not self-supporting, and it became an ordinary theatre, before it burned down shortly afterwards. Opera in New York had no permanent home until the Metropolitan Opera was built almost forty years later.

Da Ponte died on August 17, 1838 in his ninetieth year, having made his confession and received extreme unction.

Characterisation in 'Don Giovanni'

The characterisation in *Don Giovanni* has stimulated many writers to descriptive analysis. As a tiny taste of this discussion, I have selected extracts from three British authors to illustrate some of the principal characters. Other sources may be found in the bibliography. — the Editor

from E.J. Dent's *Mozart's Operas*

Elvira is by far the most interesting of the characters, after Don Giovanni himself. Anna has been made into a tragic figure by later interpreters, but it may be doubted whether she is really anything more than self-absorbed and aloof. In so far as she comes into the earlier plays, she is not tragic at all; she is simply young and very foolish, almost as inexperienced, though nowhere near so lovable, as Tatiana in Tchaikovsky's *Eugene Onegin*. She has a narrow escape, and may be thankful that at the end of Tirso's play Don Juan, with his dying breath, states definitely that she is *virgo intacta*, which cannot be said of any of the other females in it. But in da Ponte's libretto the whole situation is changed by the fact that Don Giovanni, unlike Don Juan, has no practical success with any of his so-called victims; he gets the worst of it with all three, even with Elvira, although we must pretty certainly admit that she was definitely seduced at Burgos.

Anna treats even Don Ottavio in so distant a manner that we cannot expect her to reveal her true self in any duet or trio. She seems to have been brought up from childhood always to conceal her real feelings and never acknowledge to herself any motive but duty and family pride. If she had been Italian and not Spanish, she might have been Fiordiligi in *Così fan tutte*, and there seems every probability that she will eventually become first lady-in-waiting to the Queen of the Night. She is in fact a thoroughly unpleasant young lady. Elvira, on the other hand, knows no restraints. We know from Molière, who created her, that she is an escaped nun, but that hardly justified Baudelaire in calling her *la chaste et maigre Elvire*, and the second epithet seems peculiarly inappropriate to any reader who has seen the opera in Germany (...)

With Donna Anna's long recitative and aria (*Or sai chi l'onore*) we return to tragedy for a moment. It is on this occasion above all others that we feel the utter inadequacy of Don Ottavio. We had hoped on his first appearance that his character would be developed as the opera went on; but instead of that he becomes steadily less and less interesting. Mozart seems to have been unfortunate in his Italian tenors. Kelly must have been pretty competent, but he was evidently a *tenore buffo* by temperament, to judge from his own memoirs; the sort of part that he enjoyed was the comic old prime minister in Paisiello's *Re Teodoro in Venezia*, or the poet in Righini's *Demorgorgone*, where he openly caricatured the airs and graces of da Ponte himself. The tenor Morella, who sang Don Ottavio in Vienna, was unequal to the difficulties of *Il mio tesoro*, and Mozart composed the other tenor aria for him — *Dalla sua pace*. Ottavio's inadequacy is in fact the weak point of the whole opera. It is all the more apparent in this scene with Donna Anna, for she appears here as a regular virago — more like Electra than Ilia in *Idomeneo*. The result is that in practice Ottavio's little interjections of anxiety and relief during the long story of her encounter with Don Giovanni and his attempted rape of her become positively comical, and it is noticeable that a modern English audience almost invariably receives them with ribald laughter, however earnestly he may try to ejaculate them. *Dalla sua pace*, beautiful as it is, falls very flat after the energetic outburst of Anna's exit aria. (. . .)

from Brigid Brophy's *Mozart the Dramatist* Chapter 8: Compulsive Seduction

The enlightenment had, in fact, taken the seducer for its outlaw-hero because he was the epitome of the enlightenment's own race against impotence. It was sympathetic to him because he was trapped in its own neurosis; and it execrated him because he shewed it its doom. Don Giovanni's is the fate of emancipated eighteenth-century man (. . .) Don Giovanni (exemplifying the disruptive effect of the seducer) kills a man who is presented to us dramatically in the exclusive role of a father (. . .) But he does not want to kill the Commendatore, or even fight him; he is obliged to fight in self-defence, because the Commendatore has drawn on him, and he can quite well hold himself morally guiltless of the Commendatore's death. Yet the whole point of the opera, and especially of its ending, is to hold him guilty. Let the enlightenment feel as rationally justified as it will; to kill a father-figure, even in self-defence, is a crime and breaks a taboo law; the unseen forces of the unconscious (figured in the opera as the supernatural powers of hell) will rise and exact vengeance (. . .) The enlightenment is making its point that seduction leads inevitably to more violently anti-social consequences (. . .) The enlightenment cast off the seducer precisely because he had lost the power to proceed or stop: he could no longer do what the enlightenment most admired, namely regulate his conduct rationally in order to secure his own pleasure (. . .) The theme that one crime inevitably enslaves the criminal to the next had taken on a compulsive meaning. Mozart was quite aware of this theme: in a letter to his father where he protests his own chastity and insists that if he erred he would not conceal it, he adds: 'for, after all, . . . to err once would be mere weakness — although indeed I should not undertake to promise that if I had erred in this way, I should stop short at one slip'. These words are the psychological germ of Don Giovanni; they mark Mozart's discovery in himself of potentialities out of which he was presently to create his hero.

Sexually as well as intellectually, enlightenment man had emancipated himself by reason only to become the prisoner of forces which, because they were unconscious, reason (short of a psycho-analytical theory) could not combat, and which in the end bound him to behaviour which neither reason nor self-love could endorse. The libertine is really courting not women but his own destruction. The opportunity to indulge in pleasure has turned into an obligation; the Ego is just as enslaved to hedonism as ever it was to the father-figures who imposed abstinence (. . .)

from Julian Rushton's *Don Giovanni*

Nos. 8 and 9 show the opposite poles of Elvira. In No. 8 she admonishes a peasant girl; Dent was reminded of a sermon. The style has rightly been identified as archaic, and Mozart cannot have been unaware that he was, not for the first time, composing 'in Handelian style'. When she perceives that Anna is her social equal, Elvira adopts a tone of persuasion, almost palpably getting a grip on herself at *'Non ti fidar . . . '* This owes nothing to Bertati, or Molière; nor are the words so very different from those she used to Zerlina. One could hardly find a better demonstration of the truism that in opera the composer is the dramatist.

The fascination and vividness of Elvira lie in this volatile *mezzo carattere*.

Her vehemence and tenderness emerge from the depths of love and shame, and alternate in any number long enough to accommodate both. Both sensuous and pious, she is thoroughly mixed in her motives; her interventions derive their effectiveness from jealousy as well as altruism. Her adaptability makes her like Giovanni, his complementary opposite (as Leporello is his shadow): constant in love where he is changeable, changeable in intention where he is constant. The strength of her love is her undoing and her triumph, for while it lets her be fooled it also permits the moral victory of final renunciation. There is no practical result; her feelings overwhelm her, she is incoherent, and Giovanni is amused rather than moved. But this Elvira is more human than any of her prototypes. (. . .)

The cemetery scene at Covent Garden in 1847 (Raymond Mander and Joe Mitchenson Theatre Collection)

Thematic Guide

Many of the themes from the opera have been identified in the articles by numbers in square brackets, which refer to the themes set out on these pages. The themes are also identified by the numbers in brackets at the corresponding points in the libretto, so that the words can be related to the musical themes.

[1] *Overture*

[2]

[3]

[4]

[5] **LEPORELLO** / *No. 1 Introduction*

Hot and dry, or cold and wet, wait-ing, work-ing, night and day,
Not - te e gior - no fa - ti - car, per chi nul - la sa gra - dir;

[6] **DONNA ANNA** / *No. 2 Duet*

Leave me, you're cru - el. Leave me!
Fug - gi, cru - de - le, fug - gi

42

[7] **DONNA ANNA AND DON OTTAVIO**

Allegro

We swear that we'll have ven - geance!
Che giu - ra - men - to, oh De - i!

[8] **DONNA ELVIRA** / *No. 3 Aria*

Allegro

Ah, shall I ev - er find him?
Ah! chi mi di - ce ma - i,

[9] **LEPORELLO** / *No. 4 Aria*

Allegro

Now my la - dy, here's a list of his con - quests
Ma - da - mi - na! Il ca - ta - lo - go e que - sto,

[10]

Andante con moto

With a wo - man fair - haired and youth - ful,
Nel - la bion - da e - gli ha l'u - san - za.

[11] **ZERLINA** / *No. 5 Chorus*

Allegro

When a girl finds a lov - er who's rea - dy, a lov - er who's rea - dy
Gio - vi - net - te, che fa - te all' a - mo - re, che fa - te all' a - mo - re,

[12] **MASETTO** / *No. 6 Aria*

Allegro di molto

Yes, of course, sir As you will
Ho ca - pi - to, Si - gnor, si!

[13]

Allegro di molto

As you long to be a la - dy, he will show you how to start.
Fac - cia il no - stro Ca - va - lie - re Ca - va - lie - ra an - co - ra te,

[14] **DON GIOVANNI** / *No. 7 Duettino*

Andante

There will our vows be pligh - ted, there you will an - swer 'Yes'.
La ci da - rem la ma - no, là mi di - rai di si;

[15] **ZERLINA AND DON GIOVANNI**

Allegro

We go, we go my trea - sure,
An - diam, an - diam, mio be - ne,

[16] **DONNA ELVIRA** / *No. 8 Aria*

Allegro

f Be - ware the trait - or's lies, Nor trust his flatt' ring speech!
Ah! fug - gi il tra - di - tor! Non lo la - sciar piu dir;

[17] **DONNA ELVIRA** / *No. 9 Quartet*

Andante

f No; _____ do not trust this wick - ed man!
Non _____ ti fi - dar, o mi - se - ra,

[18] **DONNA ANNA** / *No. 10 Aria*

Andante

You know now the trai - tor who sought to dis - hon - our
Or sai, chi l'o - no - re ra - pi - re a me vol - se,

[19] **DON OTTAVIO** / *No. 11 Aria*

Andantino sostenuto

p All peace and plea - sure rest in her keep - - ing
Dal - la sua pa - ce la mia_ di - pen - - de,

[20] **DON GIOVANNI** / *No. 12 Aria*

Presto

p Get them all drink - ing, Stop them from think - ing,
Fin ch' han dal vi - no cal - da la te - sta,

[21] **ZERLINA** / *No. 13 Aria*

Andante grazioso

Beat me, beat me, dear Ma - set - to, I am weak and you des - pise me.
Bat - ti, bat - ti, o bel Ma - set - to, la tua po - ve - ra Zer - li - na;

[22]

Allegretto

Let us now make peace Ma - set - to,
Pa - ce, pa - ce, o vi - ta mi - a!

[23] **MASETTO** / *No. 14 Finale*

Allegro assai

Quick - ly! quick-ly! While he's com - ing, I must find a place to hide here.
Pre - sto, pre - sto, pria ch'ei ven - ga, por - mi vo' da qual - che la - to

[24] **DONNA ELVIRA**

Allegretto

Now sum -mon all your -cour - age, the task is clear be - fore us.
Bi - so - gna a - ver co - rag - gio, o ca - ri a - mi - ci mie - i!

44

[34] **LEPORELLO** / *No. 21 Aria*

Allegro assai

Ah, have pi - ty on my fate! Ah, have pi - ty on
Ah, pie - tà! Si - gno - ri miei! Ah pie - tà, pie - tà,

[35] **DON OTTAVIO** / *No. 22 Aria*

Andante grazioso

p On your af - fec - tion re - ly - ing
Il mio te - so - ro in - tan - to

[36] **DONNA ELVIRA** / *No. 23 Aria*

Allegretto

He be - trayed the love I gave him the love I gave him.
Mi tra - dì __ quell' al - ma in - gra - ta, quell' al - ma in - gra - ta

[37] **LEPORELLO** / *No. 24 Duet*

Allegro

Most fine and no - ble mon - u - ment O great Com-men-da - to - re.
O sta - tua gen - ti - lis - si - ma del gran Com-men-da to - re.

[38] **DONNA ANNA** / *No. 25 Rondo*

Larghetto

Say no - more my heart's be - lov - ed,
Non mi ____ dir, ____ bell' i - dol mi - o,

[39] **DON GIOVANNI** / *No. 26 Finale*

Allegro vivace

p

f *p*

Now the ta - ble's laid and rea - dy.
Già la men - sa è pre - pa - ra - ta.

[40] **DONNA ELVIRA**

Allegro assai

Once more I of - fer proof of af - fec - tion,
L'ul - ti - ma pro - va dell' a - mor mi - o,

[41]

Allegro assai

p

[42] **DONNA ELVIRA, ZERLINA, DON OTTAVIO, MASETTO**

Allegro assai

f

Where is the crim - in - al?
Ah, dov' e il per - fi - do?

Don Giovanni

Dramma Giocoso in Two Acts by
Wolfgang Amadeus Mozart

Libretto by Lorenzo da Ponte
English translation by Norman Platt and Laura Sarti

Don Giovanni was first performed at the National Theatre (now known as the Tyl Theatre), Prague, on October 29, 1787. It was first performed in London at the King's Theatre, Haymarket, on April 12, 1817 (and at Covent Garden in English on May 30, 1817). The first performance in America was at the Park Theatre, New York on May 23, 1826 and, in English, in Philadelphia on November 6, 1837.

Mozart's autograph score is in the Bibliothèque de la Conservatoire de Musique in Paris. This gives the version presented in Prague in 1787. Mozart and da Ponte made a number of alterations for the first performance in Vienna in 1788, as can be seen in the printed Viennese score preserved in the Conservatorio di Firenze. Some of these have been included in the usual performing version, namely the aria *'Dalla sua pace'* and the recitative and aria *'In quali eccessi'* and *'Mi tradì'*. The other variants are noted in the text, and the additional scenes are on page 107.

In preparing this libretto of *Don Giovanni* we began with the edition made by Paolo Lecaldano for Rizzoli (*Tre libretti per Mozart*, Milan, 1956). There da Ponte's autograph version is presented with carefully systematised stage-directions, modernised and consistent spellings, and regular punctuation. The aim was to produce an accurate version of the literary text. We have varied from this where the text differs from what Mozart finally set to music. While the lay-out and stage-directions follow the original libretto as far as possible, we have reverted to certain archaisms of spelling and inserted Mozart's words in order to present what is actually sung. The stage directions have very occasionally been supplemented by those in the score, where there is no indication at all in the libretto. As such, they represent no actual production and do not form part of the translation.

The translation was extensively revised for a new production by Kent Opera in 1983.

The numbers in square brackets refer to the Thematic Guide, and the numbers in italics are the numbers in the score. The braces in the margin show where characters sing together.

THE CHARACTERS

Don Giovanni *a young and extremely licentious*	*baritone*
gentleman (giovane cavaliere estremamente licenzioso)	
Donna Anna *a lady promised in marriage to*	*soprano*
Don Ottavio	*tenor*
The Commendatore *father to Donna Anna*	*bass*
Donna Elvira *a lady of Burgos*	*soprano*
abandoned by Don Giovanni	
Leporello *Don Giovanni's servant*	*bass*
Masetto *a countryman in love with*	*bass*
Zerlina *a country girl*	*soprano*

Chorus of Countrymen and Women, Chorus of Waiters, Off-stage Chorus, Instrumentalists, Servants

The action takes place in a city of Spain

Paolo Montarsolo
(Leporello) and Kostas
Paskalis (Don Giovanni)
at Glyndebourne in 1967
(photo: Guy Gravett)

Act One

Scene One. *A garden. On one side is the Commendatore's town house, with stone benches along the walls. Night. Leporello, then Donna Anna and Don Giovanni; finally the Commendatore. / No. 1. Introduction*

LEPORELLO

Hot and dry, or cold and wet,	[5]	Notte e giorno faticar
Waiting, working, night and day,		Per chi nulla sa gradir;
Not a word of thanks I get,		Piova e vento sopportar,
Little sleep and wretched pay.		Mangiar male e mal dormir . . .
I was made for wealth and leisure,		Voglio far il gentiluomo,
Born to order, not obey!		E non voglio più servir.
There's my kind and upright master!		Oh, che caro galantuomo!
While he adds one more seduction,		Voi star dentro con la bella,
I guard him from interruption,		Ed io far la sentinella! . . .
But I hear some people coming,		Ma mi par che venga gente . . .
I don't think I ought to stay.		Non mi voglio far sentir.

(He hides.)

DONNA ANNA
(She enters, holding firmly onto Don Giovanni's arm, as he tries to shake her off.)

Shameless man, unless you kill me,	Non sperar, se non m'uccidi,
I will never let you go.	Ch'io ti lasci fuggir mai.

DON GIOVANNI

Foolish girl, despite your screaming,	Donna folle! indarno gridi:
Who I am you shall not know.	Chi son io tu non saprai.

LEPORELLO
(aside)

How she's howling! Oh, what an uproar!	Che tumulto! . . . Oh, ciel, che gridi
We're in trouble once again.	Il padron in nuovi guai!

DONNA ANNA

Father, friends and servants, hurry!	Gente! . . . servi! . . . Al traditore! . . .

DON GIOVANNI

Silence, or I'll make you sorry.	Taci, e trema al mio furore.

DONNA ANNA

Wicked monster!	Scellerato!

DON GIOVANNI

Foolish creature!	Sconsigliata!

(aside)

If I can't escape this fury,	Questa furia disperata
She will bring about my end.	Mi vuol far precipitar.

DONNA ANNA

Like a wild avenging fury	Come furia disperata
I'll pursue you to the end.	Ti saprò perseguitar.

LEPORELLO
(aside)

I'm the one who'll have to pay for	Sta' a veder che il malandrino
All his madness in the end.	Mi farà precipitar.

COMMENDATORE
(running in)

Leave her, you coward!	Lasciala, indegno!

(Hearing the Commendatore's voice, Donna Anna lets Don Giovanni go and returns into the house.)

Face me instead, sir!   Battiti meco.

DON GIOVANNI

No, fighting old men   Va': non mi degno
Gives me no pleasure!   Di pugnar teco.

COMMENDATORE

On such a pretext   Così pretendi
You'd run away?   Da me fuggir?

LEPORELLO
(aside)

On any pretext   Potessi almeno
I'd run away!   Di qua partir!

DON GIOVANNI

(Wretched man!) If you're determined,   Misero! Attendi,
Then die your way.   Se vuol morir.

(They fight. Don Giovanni deals the Commendatore a mortal wound.)

COMMENDATORE

Someone help me! He betrayed me.   Ah, soccorso! ... Son tradito ...
Now the pains of death invade me.   L'assassino ... m'ha ferito ...
From my breast my soul is flying   E dal seno ... palpitante ...
To eternal night or day.   Sento ... l'anima ... partir ...

(With this the Commendatore dies.)

DON GIOVANNI
(aside)

Ah! A mortal wound I gave him: Ah! già cadde il sciagurato ...
Now in agony he's dying.   Affannosa e agonizzante,
From his breast his soul is flying   Già dal seno palpitante
To eternal night or day.   Veggo l'anima partir.

LEPORELLO
(aside)

That was cruel! That was brutal!   Qual misfatto! qual eccesso!
And my trembling breast must mirror   Entro il sen, dallo spavento,
All his pains and mortal terror: Palpitar il cor mi sento.
I've no words to think or say.   Io non so che far, che dir.

Scene Two. *Don Giovanni and Leporello. / Recitative*

DON GIOVANNI
(sottovoce)

Leporello, are you there still?   Leporello, ove sei?

LEPORELLO

I fear that I am, and you?   Son qui, per disgrazia. E voi?

DON GIOVANNI

                         I'm here.   Son qui.

LEPORELLO

Who's dead? You or the old one?   Chi è morto? voi o il vecchio?

DON GIOVANNI

What an idiot's question! The old one.   Che domanda da bestia! Il vecchio.

LEPORELLO

                Bravo!   Bravo!
That's a fine double slaughter: Due imprese leggiadre:
Murder the father when you've ravished   Sforzar la figlia, ed ammazzar il padre.
   the daughter.

50

DON GIOVANNI

Well, he wanted it this way.	L'ha voluto: suo danno.

LEPORELLO

And Donn'Anna,	Ma Donn'Anna
Did she want it that way?	Cosa ha voluto?

DON GIOVANNI

Silence!	Taci,
You go too far. Come quickly, or	Non mi seccar! Vien meco, se non
must I teach you –	vuoi –
(threatening to beat him)	
How to behave?	Qualche cosa ancor tu.

LEPORELLO

I'll be silent, my lord, as the	Non vo' nulla, signor: non parlo
grave.	piu.

(Exeunt.)

Scene Three. *Don Ottavio, Donna Anna and servants with lights.*

DONNA ANNA
(entering, followed by Don Ottavio; resolutely)

Quickly, my father's in danger;	Ah! del padre in periglio
Oh, come quickly to help him!	In soccorso voliam.

DON OTTAVIO
(with an unsheathed sword in his hand)

My very life-blood	Tutto il mio sangue
I will shed for him if need be.	Versero, se bisogna:
But where is that vile ruffian?	Ma dov'e il scellerato?

DONNA ANNA

Just here I left him . . .	In questo loco . . .

(She sees the body.)

No. 2. Dramatic Recitative

But what terrible sight . . . Oh, God,	Ma qual mai s'offre, o Dei,
What scene of horror lies here before me?	Spettacolo funesto agli occhi miei!
O father . . . my father . . . my dearest father! . . .	Il padre! . . . padre mio! . . . mio caro padre! . . .

DON OTTAVIO

My lord! . . .	Signore! . . .

DONNA ANNA

Ah! he is dead.	Ah! l'assassino
That murderer killed him. He's bleeding . . .	Mel trucido . . . quel sangue . . .
From this wound here . . . His face too . . .	Quella piaga . . . quel volto
Shows by its pallor that all life has left him . . .	Tinto e coperto dei color di morte . . .
His heart has ceased to beat . . . hands cold as ice . . .	Ei non respira piu . . . fredde ha le membra . . .
Oh, my father, dearest father, father beloved . . .	Padre mio! . . . caro padre! . . . padre amato! . . .
I'm fainting . . . I'm dying.	Io manco . . . io moro.

(She faints.)

DON OTTAVIO

Ah, bring some help, good people, for my beloved.	Ah! soccorrete, amici, il mio tesoro.
Find quickly some smelling-salts,	Cercatemi, recatemi
And cordial to revive her. Make haste, I beg you.	Qualche odor . . . qualche spirto . . . Ah! non tardate . . .

(Exeunt two servants.)

Donn'Anna ... loved one! ... my dearest ... Her heart is breaking Under its load of sorrow!

Donn'Anna! ... sposa! ... amica! ... Il duolo estremo La meschinella uccide!

DONNA ANNA
(*coming to*)

Ah!   Ahi!

(*Re-enter the servants.*)

DON OTTAVIO

She recovers ...   Gia rinviene.
See, now her eyes are opening.   Datele nuovi aiuti.

DONNA ANNA

My father?   Padre mio!

DON OTTAVIO

Go quickly, and hide from her eyes that sight of terror:
Bear the body inside.

Celate, allontanate agli occhi suoi
Quell'oggetto d'orrore.

(*The Commendatore's body is carried off.*)

My heart's beloved, be comforted ... Take courage!

Anima mia, consolati ... fa' core!

Duet

DONNA ANNA

Heartless and cruel. Leave me!
Leave me to die beside him.
He gave me life. Oh Heaven!
And now his life is gone.

[6] Fuggi, crudele, fuggi!
Lascia che mora anch'io
Ora ch'e morto, oddio!
Chi a me la vita die.

DON OTTAVIO

Hear me, my love, oh, hear me!
Look in my eyes one moment;
Your lover shares your torment
And lives for you alone!

Senti, cor mio, deh! senti,
Guardami un solo istante:
Ti parla il caro amante
Che vive sol per te.

DONNA ANNA

Ah, yes, my love, don't leave me.
My words were madness ... forgive me!
Where can my father be?

Tu sei ... Perdon, mio bene ...
L'affanno mio ... le pene ...
Ah! il padre mio dov'e?

DON OTTAVIO

Your father? Ah, forswear
Memories too harsh to bear:
Both husband and father I'll be.

Il padre ... Lascia, o cara,
La rimembranza amara:
Hai sposo e padre in me.

Dramatic Recitative

DONNA ANNA

Swear to avenge my father,
Swear it by Heaven above!

Ah! vendicar, se il puoi,
Giura quel sangue ognor.

DON OTTAVIO

I swear it! I swear it!
By your dear eyes I swear it,
I swear by our true love.

Lo giuro! lo giuro!
Lo giuro agli occhi tuoi,
Lo giuro al nostro amor.

Duet

DONNA ANNA AND DON OTTAVIO

O night of grief and terror
Our dreadful oath attending!
Within our hearts contending
Vengeance and sorrow move.

[7] Che giuramento, o Dei!
Che barbaro momento!
Tra cento affetti e cento
Vammi ondeggiando il cor.

(*Exeunt.*)

Scene Four. *A street. Dawn. Don Giovanni and Leporello.* / *Recitative*

DON GIOVANNI

Well then, what is it this time? Tell me   Orsù, spicciati presto ... Cosa vuoi?
quickly.

LEPORELLO

The matter I would speak of   L'affar di cui si tratta
Is most important.   È importante.

DON GIOVANNI

I believe you.   Lo credo.

LEPORELLO

Of the utmost importance.   È importantissimo.

DON GIOVANNI

I'm delighted: get on with it.   Meglio ancora: finiscila.

LEPORELLO

You promise   Giurate
You will not lose your temper?   Di non andar in collera.

DON GIOVANNI

I swear it on my honour,   Lo giuro sul mio onore:
Unless you mention the Commendatore.   Purché non parli del Commendatore.

LEPORELLO

We're alone?   Siamo soli?

DON GIOVANNI

As you see.   Lo vedo.

LEPORELLO

There's no-one listening?   Nessun ci sente ...

DON GIOVANNI

No!   Via!

LEPORELLO

And I'm allowed   Vi posso dire
To speak my mind quite freely?   Tutto liberamente ...

DON GIOVANNI

Yes.   Sì!

LEPORELLO

I just wanted to say ...   Dunque, quand'è così:
(He speaks into his ear, but aloud.)
I know you won't mind, Sir.   Caro signor padrone,
The life you are leading is that of a   La vita che menate è da briccone!
swine, Sir!

DON GIOVANNI

How dare you? You insolent ...   Temerario! In tal guisa ...

LEPORELLO

You gave your oath ...   E il giuramento ...

DON GIOVANNI

What oath? I don't remember. Be quiet   Non so di giuramento ... Taci ... o
before ...   ch'io ...

LEPORELLO

I understand. I won't say any more.   Non parlo più, non fiato, o padron mio.

In that case we'll be friends again. Listen to me now!
Why do you think I'm here?

Così saremo amici. Or odi un poco:
Sai tu perche son qui?

LEPORELLO

I can't imagine.
But since a new day's breaking, some new woman
Must be here for the taking.
Could you give me her name for the list I'm making?

Non ne so nulla.
Ma, essendo l'alba chiara, non sarebbe
Qualche nuova conquista?
Io lo devo saper per porla in lista.

DON GIOVANNI

Well done; you know it all! But I must tell you
That I'm in love with a beautiful creature,
And I'm sure she loves me.
I've seen her, we've spoken – and tonight she will come
To my house of pleasure. Hush I'm certain
I caught a scent of woman there!

Va' la che sei il grand'uom! Sappi ch'io sono
Innamorato d'una bella dama;
E son certo che m'ama.
La vidi, le parlai; meco al casino
Questa notte verra . . . Zitto: mi pare
Sentir odor di femmina . . .

LEPORELLO

Good heavens!
What a fine sense of smell!

Cospetto!
Che odorato perfetto!

DON GIOVANNI

I'd say that she was beautiful . . .

All'aria mi par bella.

LEPORELLO
(*aside*)

You've fine sight as well.

E che occhio, dico!

DON GIOVANNI

She may need our assistance.
Let us hide here and observe her.

Ritiriamoci un poco,
E scopriamo terren.

LEPORELLO

On fire to serve her.

Gia prese fuoco.

Scene Five. *Don Giovanni, Leporello and Donna Elvira. / No. 3. Aria*

DONNA ELVIRA
(*entering in her travelling clothes*)

Ah, shall I ever find him?
Who broke my heart in play.
Nor faith nor love could bind him,
He cast them both away.
Ah, should he stand before me
And still my claim deny,
With my own hands I'd kill him,
And laugh to see him die!

[8] Ah! chi mi dice mai
Quel barbaro dov'e,
Che per mio scorno amai,
Che mi manco di fè?
Ah! se ritrovo l'empio,
E a me non torna ancor,
Vo' farne orrendo scempio,
Gli vo' cavar il cor.

DON GIOVANNI
(*sottovoce to Leporello*)

How dreadful! One so lovely,
Seduced and then abandoned. Poor young lady!
We really ought to comfort and console her.

Udisti? Qualche bella
Dal vago abbandonata. Poverina!
Cerchiam di consolare il suo tormento.

LEPORELLO
(*aside*)

With eighteen hundred others I'll enrol her.

Così ne consolò mille e ottocento.

DON GIOVANNI

Signorina.   Signorina.

Recitative

DONNA ELVIRA

Who's that?   Chi è la?

DON GIOVANNI

Heaven preserve us!   Stelle! che vedo!

LEPORELLO

Delicious Donn'Elvira!   Oh, bella! Donn'Elvira!

DONNA ELVIRA

Don Giovanni!   Don Giovanni! ...
You here? Vilest of men! Monster   Sei qui, mostro, fellon, nido
of wickedness.   d'inganni ...

LEPORELLO
(aside)

She knows how to address him! But of   Che titoli cruscanti! Manco male
course
They were closely acquainted.   Che lo conosce bene.

DON GIOVANNI

Come now, dear Donn'Elvira,   Via, cara Donn'Elvira,
Do not give way to bitterness ... just   Calmate questa collera ... sentite ...
listen ...
Allow me to speak.   Lasciatemi parlar ...

DONNA ELVIRA

And what could you   Cosa puoi dire,
Say, after the way you acted? You wormed Dopo azion si nera? In casa mia
your way
Into my home and my affections, and by   Entri furtivamente. A forza d'arte,
your cunning
With solemn oaths and flattering words   Di giuramenti e di lusinghe, arrivi
you succeeded
In seducing my heart   A sedurre il cor mio:
And in making me love you.   M'innamori, o crudele,
You promised me marriage, then in   Mi dichiari tua sposa. E poi, mancando
defiance
Of the most sacred rights of earth and   Della terra e del cielo al santo dritto,
Heaven,
O despicable creature!   Con enorme delitto
After three days you went away from   Dopo tre di da Burgos t'allontani,
Burgos,
You deceived me, ran away, and left me   M'abbandoni, mi fuggi, e lasci in preda
the prey
Of remorse and weeping,   Al rimorso ed al pianto,
To pay the price of loving you too well. Per pena forse che t'amai cotanto.

LEPORELLO
(aside)

She ought to write a book on it.   Pare un libro stampato.

DON GIOVANNI

But I assure you   Oh, in quanto a questo
I had the strongest reasons.   Ebbi le mie ragioni.
(to Leporello)
You'll confirm that?   È vero?

LEPORELLO

Oh, yes, Sir ...   È vero.
(with irony)
Private and personal reasons.   È che ragioni forti! ...

55

DONNA ELVIRA

And what could they be?
Apart from your deceit
And your irresponsibility? But Heaven is
just,
And willed it that I should find you
To wreak its vengeance and my own too.

E quali sono,
Se non la tua perfidia,
La leggerezza tua? Ma il giusto cielo
Volle ch'io ti trovassi
Per far le sue, le mie vendette.

DON GIOVANNI

Oh, come now,
Let us try to be reasonable.

Eh, via,
Siate piu ragionevole ...

(aside)

This woman
Is driving me mad.

Mi pone
A cimento, costei.

(to Donna Elvira)

If you will not accept
What I say, you must believe
This honest fellow.

Se non credete
Al labbro mio, credete
A questo galantuomo.

LEPORELLO
(aside)

That's a new one.

Salvo il vero.

DON GIOVANNI
(to Leporello)

Go on, you tell her.

Via, dille un poco ...

LEPORELLO
(sottovoce to Don Giovanni)

And what am I to tell her?

E cosa devo dirle?

DON GIOVANNI
(aloud, and leaving without being noticed)

Yes, yes, tell her the whole truth.

Si, si, dille pur tutto.

DONNA ELVIRA
(to Leporello)

Well then, tell me quickly.

Ebben, fa' presto.

LEPORELLO

Dear madam ... to speak the truth, and
I would swear it,
Throughout the world a circle's round
And never been a square yet.

Madama ... veramente ... in questo mondo
Conciossiacosaquandofosseché
Il quadro non é tondo ...

DONNA ELVIRA

Oh you scoundrel!
How could you use my grief only to mock
me?

Sciagurato!
Cosi del mio dolor gioco ti prendi?

(turning towards Don Giovanni, who she thinks is still there)

Ah you ...

Ah, voi ...

(realising that he has gone)

Heavens! The wretch
Has run away. What shall I do? Where now
has he gone?

Stelle! L'iniquo
Fuggi, misera me! ... Dove? in qual
parte ...

LEPORELLO

Oh ... just let him go. He isn't worth
Wasting a thought on.

Eh! lasciate che vada. Egli non merta
Che di lui ci pensiate ...

DONNA ELVIRA

That wicked man
Has deceived and betrayed me.

Il scellerato
M'ingannò, mi tradi ...

LEPORELLO

Ah, don't torment yourself.
You don't suppose, I hope, that you're the
first one?

Eh! consolatevi:
Non siete voi, non foste e non sarete

Or that you'll be the last of them? This book here –	Ne la prima ne l'ultima. Guardate
Not such a small one, is it? – This book contains	Questo non picciol libro: e tutto pieno
The names of all his conquests.	Dei nomi di sue belle.
Every village, every town, every city and nation	Ogni villa, ogni borgo, ogni paese
Offers some proof of his firm dedication.	È testimon di sue donnesche imprese.

No. 4. Aria

Little lady, here's a list of his conquests.	[9]	Madamina, il catalogo e questo
Though my master provided the action,		Delle belle che amo il padron mio;
Just to write it gave me satisfaction.		Un catalogo egli e che ho fatt'io:
It's amazing, come read it with me.		Osservate, leggete con me.

First, six hundred and forty Italians,	In Italia seicento e quaranta,
Then the Germans with two small battalions,	In Lamagna duecento e trentuna,
French one hundred, and Turks over ninety,	Cento in Francia, in Turchia novantuna,
But the Spaniards number already one thousand and three.	Ma in Ispagna son gia mille e tre.

Country wenches rate an entry,	V'han fra queste contadine,
Burghers' wives and lower gentry,	Cameriere, cittadine,
Baronesses and princesses	V'han contesse, baronesse,
Swell the ranks of his successes;	Marchesane, principesse,
Every shape of female figure,	E v'han donne d'ogni grado,
Every class and every age.	D'ogni forma, d'ogni eta.

Is a woman, fair-haired and youthful?	[10]	Nella bionda egli ha l'usanza
His approach is sentimental.		Di lodar la gentilezza;
He calls dark ones wise and truthful;		Nella bruna, la costanza;
Shy and pale ones, sweet and gentle.		Nella bianca, la dolcezza.

In the cold he likes them ample,	Vuol d'inverno la grassotta,
Summer brings a thinner sample.	Vuol d'estate la magrotta;
Tall and wide he calls them stately,	È la grande maestosa,
But the tiny intrigue him greatly.	La piccina e ognor vezzosa.

Old and ugly? He can't resist them:	Delle vecchie fa conquista
He must conquer, and I must list them.	Pel piacer di porle in lista:
But his appetite is greater	Ma passion predominante
When he can initiate her.	È la giovin principiante.

Young, delicious, coarse and vicious,	Non si picca se sia ricca,
Sleazy slut or lovely creature,	Se sia brutta, se sia bella:
If she's female in each feature,	Purchè porti la gonnella,
You could teach her what he'll do.	Voi sapete quel che fa.

(*Exit.*)

Scene Six. *Donna Elvira alone.* / *Recitative*

DONNA ELVIRA

And so Don Giovanni	In questa forma, dunque,
Has deceived and betrayed me. Thus he rewards me	Mi tradi il scellerato? È questo il premio
For the loving affection that I gave him.	Che quel barbaro rende all'amor mio?
Ah, I will take my vengeance.	Ah, vendicar vogl'io
He's rejected my love. He shan't escape me.	L'ingannato mio cor: pria ch'ei mi fugga ...
I'll pursue him and find him. My heart is raging	Si ricorra ... si vada ... Io sento in petto
With a bitter despair, anger, and resentment.	Sol vendetta parlar, rabbia e dispetto.

(*Exit.*)

Scene Seven. *The country close to Don Giovanni's mansion. Zerlina, Masetto, peasant men and women. / No. 5. Chorus*

ZERLINA

When a girl finds a lover who's ready, [11]
She should not waste her time in delay.
When her heart is aflame and her pulse
  is unsteady,
Then the remedy lies in her way.
Ah, ah, ah; ah, ah, ah!
Let her marry as soon as she may.

Giovinette che fate all'amore,
Non lasciate che passi l'età:
Se nel seno vi bulica il core,

Il rimedio vedetelo qua.
Ah, ah, ah; ah, ah, ah!
Che piacer, che piacer che sarà!

CHORUS OF PEASANT WOMEN

Ah, ah, ah; ah, ah, ah!
Let her marry as soon as she may.
La la la re la, la la la re la.

Ah, ah, ah; ah, ah, ah!
Che piacer, che piacer che sarà!
La la la re la, la la la re la.

MASETTO

All you men whose affections may
  wander,
And who spend all your leisure in play
  and stray,
The result of stupidity ponder
And from me learn some wisdom today.
Ah, ah, ah; ah, ah, ah!
Just get married as soon as you may.

Giovinotti leggeri di testa,

Non andate girando di qua e là;

Poco dura de' matti la festa,
Ma per me cominciato non ha.
Ah, ah, ah; ah, ah, ah!
Che piacer, che piacer che sarà!

CHORUS OF MEN

Ah, ah, ah; ah, ah, ah!
Just get married as soon as you may.
La la la re la, la la la re la!

Ah, ah, ah; ah, ah, ah!
Che piacer, che piacer che sarà!
La la la re la, la la la re la!

ZERLINA, MASETTO

As the hour of our wedding advances,

We will greet it with singing and dances:

As the hour of our wedding advances,

We are happy and happy we'll stay.
Ah, ah, ah; ah, ah, ah!
We are happy and happy we'll stay.

Vieni, vieni, carin{o, /a, godiamo,

E cantiamo e balliamo e saltiamo;

Vieni, vieni, carin{o, /a, godiamo,

Che piacer, che piacer che sarà!
Ah, ah, ah; ah, ah, ah!
Che piacer, che piacer che sarà!

Scene Eight. *Zerlina, Masetto, peasant men and women, Don Giovanni, and Leporello. / Recitative*

DON GIOVANNI
(*entering, aside*)

Well, at least we're rid of her.
        (*aside to Leporello*)
        But look now, look now,
At all these fine young people, these lovely
  women!

Manco male, è partita.

                Oh, guarda, guarda
Che bella gioventù, che belle donne!

LEPORELLO
(*aside*)

Among such a crowd
I might even find one or two for myself.

Tra tante, per mia fè,
Vi sarà qualche cosa anche per me.

DON GIOVANNI

Friends, I bid you good morning. But
  please
Don't let me interrupt you.
Continue to enjoy yourselves, good people.
Is there to be a wedding?

Cari amici, buongiorno. Seguitate

A stare allegramente,
Seguitate a suonar, o buona gente.
C'è qualche sposalizio?

ZERLINA

Yes, indeed, Sir.
And I'm to be the bride.

Si, signore;
E la sposa son io.

DON GIOVANNI

Well, how delightful.
And the bridegroom?

Me ne consolo.
Lo sposo?

MASETTO

Me, at your service.

Io, per servirla.

DON GIOVANNI

How splendid! At my service. Now those
are the words
Of an honest fellow.

Oh, bravo! per servirmi: questo è vero

Parlar da galantuomo!

LEPORELLO
(aside)

Let's hope he reaches the church.

Basta che sia marito!

ZERLINA

Oh, my Masetto's
A true hearted man, sir.

Oh! il mio Masetto
È un uom d'ottimo core.

DON GIOVANNI

Oh, so am I.
I hope we shall be friends soon. What is
your name, child?

Oh, anch'io, vedete!
Voglio che siamo amici. Il vostro nome?

ZERLINA

Zerlina.

Zerlina.

DON GIOVANNI

And yours?

E il tuo?

MASETTO

Masetto.

Masetto.

DON GIOVANNI

My dear young friend Masetto,
And my dear friend Zerlina, I must take
you
Both under my protection.

Oh, caro il mio Masetto!
Cara la mia Zerlina! V'esibisco

La mia protezione.

(To Leporello, who is joking with the other peasant women.)

Leporello, scoundrel, what are you doing?
doing?

Leporello ... cosa fai lì, birbone?

LEPORELLO

I too, my dear master,
Am just showing these girls my protection.

Anch'io, caro padrone,
Esibisco la mia protezione.

DON GIOVANNI

Now be off with you at once, and show
these people
The way to my palace. See they
have plenty
To eat and drink, order wine, chocolate,
and coffee.
Make sure everyone's happy,
Show them all round the garden;
Show them the gallery, the apartments,
and take special care
To amuse my good friend Masetto.
You understand?

Presto, va' con costor: nel mio palazzo

Conducili sul fatto. Ordina
ch'abbiano
Cioccolatte, caffè, vini, prosciutti.

Cerca divertir tutti:
Mostra loro il giardino,
La galleria, le camere; in effetto,

Fa' che resti contento il mio Masetto.
Hai capito?

LEPORELLO

I understand.

Ho capito.

Come along.   Andiam.

MASETTO
(to Don Giovanni)

My lord . . .   Signore . . .

DON GIOVANNI

Well, what now?   Cosa c'è?

MASETTO

My Zerlina   La Zerlina
Can't stay here without me.   Senza me non può star.

LEPORELLO

But she'll be quite safe   In vostro loco
In the hands of his lordship. He can   Vi sarà sua Eccellenza, e saprà bene
relieve you
Of your responsibilities.   Fare le vostre parti.

DON GIOVANNI

Yes, your Zerlina   Oh! la Zerlina
Will be in noble hands. Just go, I'll bring   È in man d'un cavalier. Va' pur: fra poco
her
Along with me soon.   Ella meco verrà.

ZERLINA

Go! Don't be frightened;   Va', non temere:
I shall be in the hands of a gentleman.   Nelle mani son io d'un cavaliere.

MASETTO

And that means?   E per questo?

ZERLINA

And that means   E per questo
That you need have no doubts.   Non c'è da dubitar . . .

MASETTO

I'm damned if I will.   Ed io, cospetto . . .

DON GIOVANNI

Enough, no more argument! This final   Olà, finiam le dispute: se subito,
Friendly warning I shall give so don't forget   Senz'altro replicar, non te ne vai,
it.
(indicating his sword)
Masetto, watch your step, or you'll regret it.   Masetto, guarda ben, ti pentirai.

No. 6. Aria

MASETTO

Yes, of course, Sir! As you will!   [12]   Ho capito, signor, sì!
I must bow and go away.   Chino il capo e me ne vò:
All your wishes I'll fulfil.   Giacchè piace a voi così,
I would never disobey.   Altre repliche non fo.

You're a gentleman, I know,   Cavalier voi siete già,
As your actions plainly show.   Dubitar non posso, affè;
When you ask me to depart,   Me lo dice la bontà
You've my interests at heart.   Che volete aver per me.
(sottovoce to Zerlina)
Little wanton, you degrade me,   Bricconaccia, malandrina,
For the last time you've betrayed me.   Fosti ognor la mia ruina.
(to Leporello, who is trying to lead him off)
Yes, I'm going.   Vengo, vengo!
(to Zerlina)
I must leave you.   Resta, resta!
Who would dare to disbelieve you?   È una cosa molto onesta:
Since you long to be a lady,   [13]   Faccia il nostro cavaliere
He will show you how to start.   Cavaliera ancora te.
(Exit Leporello with Masetto and the other peasants.)

60

Scene Nine. *Don Giovanni and Zerlina.* / *Recitative*

DON GIOVANNI

We're rid of him at last,	Alfin siamo liberati,
My sweet Zerlina. The stupid peasant!	Zerlinetta gentil, da quel scioccone.
And I managed it well, don't you agree?	Che ne dite, mio ben, so far pulito?

ZERLINA

My lord, he's to be my husband ...	Signore, è mio marito ...

DON GIOVANNI

Who? That lout?	Chi! colui?
You think an honest man,	Vi par che un onest'uomo,
A nobleman like me, if I may say so,	Un nobil cavalier, qual io mi vanto,
Could ever suffer such a charming face,	Possa soffrir che quel visetto d'oro,
Such beauty and sweetness,	Quel viso inzuccherato,
To be abused by that coarse, low-born creature?	Da un bifolcaccio vil sia strapazzato?

ZERLINA

But my lord, I have given	Ma, signor, io gli diedi
My promise to marry him.	Parola di sposarlo.

DON GIOVANNI

Such a promise	Tal parola
Can have no meaning. You were not intended	Non vale un zero. Voi non siete fatta
To live as a peasant; a different fate	Per esser paesana: un' altra sorte
I can read in those eyes so revealing,	Vi procuran quegli occhi bricconcelli,
In those lips so appealing,	Quei labbretti sì belli,
And in those little fingers soft and tender,	Quelle ditucce candide e odorose ...
Whose fragrance delights me, whose touch invites me.	Parmi toccar giuncata e fiutar rose.

ZERLINA

I should not like to ...	Ah! ... non vorrei ...

DON GIOVANNI

You would not like to ... ?	Che non vorreste?

ZERLINA

... Discover	... Alfine
You'd deceived me in the end. I have been told	Ingannata restar. Io so che raro
That men like you, men of rank and high position,	Colle donne voi altri cavalieri
Often lead girls to perdition.	Siete onesti e sinceri.

DON GIOVANNI

Oh, what a slander!	Eh, un'impostura
A plebian invention. High birth and virtue	Della gente plebea! La nobiltà
Go together; you can see it in our eyes.	Ha dipinta negli occhi l'onestà.
We've wasted time enough. This very moment	Orsù non perdiam tempo: in questo istante
I would make you my wife.	Io ti voglio sposar.

ZERLINA

You?	Voi!

DON GIOVANNI

Certainly!	Certo, io.
Come to my little summer-house. No-one will find us,	Quel casinetto è mio: soli saremo,
And there, my precious jewel, our vows shall bind us.	E là, gioiello mio, ci sposeremo.

No. 7. Duet

There will our faith be plighted,	[14]	Là ci darem la mano,
There will you answer 'Yes'.		Là mi dirai di sì.
Passion shall be requited,		Vedi, non è lontano:
And Heaven our union bless.		Partiam, ben mio, da qui.

ZERLINA
(aside)

To yield or to refuse him?	Vorrei, e non vorrei . . .
To doubt or to believe?	Mi trema un poco il cor . . .
I should not like to lose him . . .	Felice, è ver, sarei;
But still he may deceive.	Ma può burlarmi ancor.

DON GIOVANNI

Pleasure and wealth I offer.	Vieni, mio bel diletto!

ZERLINA
(aside)

And must Masetto suffer?	Mi fa pietà Masetto.

DON GIOVANNI

Come then, be poor no longer.	Io cangerò tua sorte.

ZERLINA
(aside)

Ah, would that I were stronger.	Presto non son più forte.

DON GIOVANNI

Come then, come then!	Vieni, vieni.

(They repeat their verses.)

DON GIOVANNI

You will, you will!	Andiam, andiam!

ZERLINA

I will!	Andiam!

ZERLINA AND DON GIOVANNI

We go, we go my treasure,	[15]	Andiam, andiam, mio bene,
To share the lasting pleasure		A ristorar le pene
That innocent love can give.		D'un innocente amor!

(They go off, arm in arm, towards Don Giovanni's summer-house.*)

Scene Ten. *Don Giovanni, Zerlina and Donna Elvira. / Recitative*

DONNA ELVIRA
(She enters, and stops Don Giovanni with frenzied gestures.)

Stop, wicked man, and leave her! Heaven sent me	Fermati, scellerato! Il ciel mi fece
Just in time to hear your treachery, that I might rescue	Udir le tue perfidie. Io sono a tempo
And preserve this innocent young creature	Di salvar questa misera innocente
From your barbarous clutches.	Dal tuo barbaro artiglio.

ZERLINA

His treachery! What does this mean?	Meschina! Cosa sento!

DON GIOVANNI
(aside)

Love now inspire me!	Amor, consiglio!

(sottovoce to Donna Elvira)

My beloved, this is merely	Idol mio, non vedete
A passing diversion.	Ch'io voglio divertirmi?

---

* i.e. 'casino' as opposed to his 'palazzo' (here translated as mansion)

DONNA ELVIRA
(aloud)

A diversion!
Yes, that's true! A diversion! I know too well
Just what you mean by diversion.

Divertirti,
È vero! divertirti . . . Io so, crudele,
Come tu ti diverti.

ZERLINA

But my Lord, do please tell me
If what she says is true.

Ma, signor cavaliere,
È ver quel ch'ella dice?

DON GIOVANNI
(sottovoce to Zerlina)

This poor unhappy woman
Is in love with me madly,
So when I meet her I humour her blindness,
Since one of my few failings is too much kindness.

La povera infelice
È di me innamorata,
E per pietà deggio fingere amore,
Ch'io son, per mia disgrazia, uom di buon core.

No. 8. Aria

DONNA ELVIRA
(to Zerlina)

Beware the traitor's lies,
Nor trust his flattering speech!
Deceiving are his eyes
And false his wooing.

[16]

Ah, fuggi il traditor,
Non lo lasciar più dir:
Il labbro è mentitor,
Fallace il ciglio.

Too late I learnt by suffering
Of stone his heart is made.
Avoid the price I paid
Or share my ruin.

Da' miei tormenti impara
A creder a quel cor.
E nasca il tuo timor
Dal mio periglio.

(Exit, taking Zerlina with her.)

Scene Eleven. *Don Giovanni; then Donna Anna and Don Ottavio. / Recitative*

DON GIOVANNI

I think today the devil's own diversion is
To destroy my pleasure and amusement.
All my plans come to nothing.

Mi par ch'oggi il demonio si diverta
D'opporsi a' miei piacevoli progressi!
Vanno mal tutti quanti.

DON OTTAVIO
(entering with Donna Anna, and addressing her)

Consider, my beloved, all tears are useless.
Let us rather think of vengeance . . . Ah, Don Giovanni.

Ah! ch'ora, idolo mio, son vani i pianti:
Di vendetta si parli . . . Ah, Don Giovanni!

DON GIOVANNI
(aside)

This I might have been spared.

Mancava questo, inver!

DONNA ANNA
(to Don Giovanni)

My friend, this meeting
Is timely. Can you feel pity? Have you
A brave and generous heart?

Signore, a tempo
Vi ritroviam: avete core, avete
Anima generosa?

DON GIOVANNI
(aside)

Can it be that
The devil has suggested something to her?
(to Donna Anna)
What a question! But why?

Sta' a vedere
Che il diavolo gli ha detto qualche cosa.

Che domanda! Perchè?

DONNA ANNA

We stand in grave need
Of your friendly assistance.

Bisogno abbiamo
Della vostra amicizia.

63

DON GIOVANNI
(aside)

In that case I can breathe again.	Mi torna il fiato in corpo.

(to Donna Anna, passionately)

Pray command me.	Comandate:
My household, my relations,	I congiunti, i parenti,
My own hand, my own sword, all my goods,	Questa man, questo ferro, i beni, il sangue
my heart's blood,	
I will offer to serve you.	Spenderò per servirvi.
But why, fairest Donn'Anna,	Ma voi, bella Donn'Anna,
Why must I find you weeping?	Perchè così piangete?
Tell me who is the wretch who could distress	Il crudele chi fu che osò la calma
One so kind, or wish to hurt her?	Turbar del viver vostro . . .

Scene Twelve. *Don Giovanni, Donna Anna, Don Ottavio and Donna Elvira.*

DONNA ELVIRA
(entering, to Don Giovanni)

I find you once again! Shameless deserter!	Ah, ti ritrovo ancor, perfido mostro!

(to Donna Anna)

No. 9. Quartet

Poor wretched woman, trust him not!	[17] Non ti fidar, o misera,
He's deaf to honour's name.	Di quel ribaldo cor.
My heart already he betrayed.	Me già tradì, quel barbaro:
Your fate would be the same.	Te vuol tradir ancor.

DONNA ANNA AND DON OTTAVIO
(aside)

Heavens! What grief and dignity!	Cieli, che aspetto nobile!
A sweet and noble face!	Che dolce maestà!
Her cheeks so pale, her weeping eyes,	Il suo pallor, le lagrime,
Cry for compassion's grace.	M'empiono di pietà.

DON GIOVANNI

The poor girl is demented,	La povera ragazza
These fits can't be prevented,	È pazza, amici miei:
I'll try to reassure her:	Lasciatemi con lei,
Leave me alone to cure her.	Forse si calmerà.
I understand her ways.	Forse si calmerà.

DONNA ELVIRA
(to Donna Anna and Don Ottavio)

Ah, do not trust his lying words!	Ah, non credete al perfido!

DON GIOVANNI

She's mad, you must believe me.	È pazza, non badate . . .

DONNA ELVIRA
(as before)

I beg you, do not leave me.	Restate, ancor restate . . .

DONNA ANNA AND DON OTTAVIO

Which one the truth betrays?	A chi si crederà?

DONNA ANNA, DON OTTAVIO AND DON GIOVANNI
(aside)

I'm / They're } beginning to feel a suspicion	Certo moto d'ignoto tormento
That this unhappy woman's position	Dentro l'alma girare mi sento,
Hides a mystery { we / they } don't understand yet,	Che mi dice per quella infelice
But the truth { we'll / they'll } endeavour to trace.	Cento cose che intender non sa.

DONNA ELVIRA

Anger, sorrow, and raging suspicion	Sdegno, rabbia, dispetto, tormento
Brought my poor heart to this wild condition;	Dentro l'alma girare mi sento,
That he's lying they don't understand yet,	Che mi dice di quel traditore
But the truth in the end they will trace.	Cento cose che intender non sa.

DON OTTAVIO
(aside)

From this place I will not stir,	Io di qua non vado via,
Unless some certainty I reach.	Se non scopro questo affar.

DONNA ANNA
(aside)

I can find no sign of madness	Non ha l'aria di pazzia
In her face or in her speech.	Il suo volto, il suo parlar.

DON GIOVANNI
(aside)

To escape now would be simply	Se men vado, si potria
To confirm the doubts of each.	Qualche cosa sospettar.

DONNA ELVIRA

See those guilty looks themselves	Da quel ceffo si dovria
The guilty soul within impeach.	La ner'alma giudicar.

DON OTTAVIO
(to Don Giovanni)

Her pretence is ...	Dunque, quella ...

DON GIOVANNI

She's lost her senses.	È pazzarella.

DONNA ANNA
(to Donna Elvira)

He deceived you?	Dunque, quegli ...

DONNA ELVIRA

There's no denying.	È un traditore.

DON GIOVANNI

Poor young woman!	Infelice!

DONNA ELVIRA

He is lying!	Mentitore!

DONNA ANNA AND DON OTTAVIO

All my doubts begin to grow.	Incomincio a dubitar.

DON GIOVANNI
(sottovoce to Donna Elvira)

Do be quiet now, confound you,	Zitto, zitto! chè la gente
Try to use a little prudence,	Si raduna a noi d'intorno.
Or you'll have a crowd around you,	Siate un poco più prudente:
And your shame the world will know.	Vi farete criticar.

DONNA ELVIRA
(aloud to Don Giovanni)

Do not think you can prevent me!	Non sperarlo, o scellerato:
Do not speak to me of prudence!	Ho perduto la prudenza.
For a witness Heaven sent me	Le tue colpe ed il mio stato
All your wickedness to show.	Voglio a tutti palesar.

DONNA ANNA AND DON OTTAVIO
(looking at Don Giovanni)

See his angry agitation,	Quegli accenti si sommessi,
See the way his colour changes,	Quel cangiarsi di colore,

Unbelief and hesitation
Soon the truth will overthrow.

Son indizi troppo espressi
Che mi fan determinar.

(*Exit Donna Elvira.*)

Recitative

DON GIOVANNI

Poor unhappy woman. I dare not leave her
In such distress. I fear
That she may do something foolish.
So forgive me, most beautiful Donn'Anna,
If I can ever serve you,
Call upon me at once. My friends, I leave you.

Povera sventurata! I passi suoi
Voglio seguir: non voglio
Che faccia un precipizio.
Perdonate, bellissima Donn'Anna:
Se servirvi poss'io,
In mia casa v'aspetto. Amici, addio!

(*Exit.*)

Scene Thirteen. *Donna Anna and Don Ottavio. / No. 10. Dramatic Recitative*

DONNA ANNA

Don Ottavio, oh, help me!

Don Ottavio . . . son morta!

DON OTTAVIO

What has happened?

Cosa è stato?

DONNA ANNA

Help me now, oh, I beg of you!

Per pietà, soccorretemi!

DON OTTAVIO

My dear,
Take courage and tell me.

Mio bene,
Fate coraggio!

DONNA ANNA

I know it! I know it! That is the murderer
Of my dear father.

Oh, Dei! Oh, Dei! Quegli è il carnefice
Del padre mio . . .

DON OTTAVIO

What are you saying?

Che dite!

DONNA ANNA

No room for doubt remains. The words he
spoke then –
The tone of his voice as he was leaving –
They recalled to my memory that vile one
Who entered my apartments . . .

Non dubitate più: gli ultimi accenti
Che l'empio proferì tutta la voce
Richiamar nel cor mio di quell' indegno
Che nel mio appartamento . . .

DON OTTAVIO

Oh, Heaven! How could a man
Beneath the sacred cloak of friendship do
such . . .
But tell it all. Describe
That strange event just as it happened.

Oh, ciel! Possibile
Che sotto il sacro manto d'amicizia . . .
Ma come fu, narratemi,
Lo strano avvenimento.

DONNA ANNA

Darkness had fallen.
It was late in the evening
When into my apartments, where by
misfortune
I was sitting alone, there came a man
With his cloak wrapped close around him,
A man who, for a moment,
I believed to be you.
But very soon I knew
That I had been mistaken . . .

Era già alquanto
Avanzata la notte,
Quando nelle mie stanze, ove soletta
Mi trovai per sventura, entrar io vidi
In un mantello avvolto
Un uom che al primo istante
Avea preso per voi:
Ma riconobbi poi
Che un inganno era il mio . . .

DON OTTAVIO
(*agitated*)

How dreadful! What happened?

Stelle! . . . Seguite.

Silently he approaches	Tacito a me s'appressa,
And attempts to embrace me. I try to free myself.	E mi vuole abbracciar; scioglermi cerco,
He holds me closer, I cry out –	Ei più mi stringe; io grido:
But no-one comes. He lays one hand upon my mouth	Non viene alcun. Con una mano cerca
To stifle my cries.	D'impedire la voce,
With the other he grips me	E coll'altra m'afferra
More tightly . . . I feel that I am conquered.	Stretta cosi, che già mi credo vinta.

DON OTTAVIO

Horrible! But then . . .	Perfido! . . . E alfin? . . .

DONNA ANNA

But then the pain, the horror	Alfine il duol, l'orrore
Of my terrible danger	Dell'infame attentato
Increased the power of my resistance –	Accrebbe si la lena mia, che, a forza
And so by turning and twisting, wriggling, fighting fiercely,	Di svincolarmi, torcermi e piegarmi,
I struggled from him.	Da lui mi sciolsi.

DON OTTAVIO

Oh God! I thank Thee!	Ohimè! respiro.

DONNA ANNA

And then	Allora
I begin to scream more loudly, crying for help.	Rinforzo i stridi miei, chiamo soccorso.
He takes to flight, and boldly I pursue him	Fugge il fellon. Arditamente il seguo
Into the street to prevent him escaping,	Fin nella strada per fermarlo, e sono
Becoming the assailer of my assailant. My father	Assalitrice d'assalita! Il padre
Comes running and demands his name, and that vile one,	V'accorre, vuol conoscerlo; e l'iniquo,
So much stronger than the old man who would pursue him,	Che del povero vecchio era più forte,
Crowned all his evil actions, attacked him and slew him!	Compie il misfatto suo col dargli morte.

Aria

You know now the traitor	[18]	Or sai chi l'onore
Who sought to dishonour		Rapire a me volse,
Your faithful beloved,		Chi fu il traditore,
And brought grief upon her.		Che il padre mi tolse.
The vengeance I call for,		Vendetta ti chieggio;
Your heart must inspire.		La chiede il tuo cor.
Remember my father.		Fammenta la piaga
In death he lay bleeding.		Del misero seno,
Remember his dear eyes		Rimira di sangue
In death still for vengeance were pleading:		Coperto il terreno,
Both anger and sorrow		Se l'ira in te langue
Your spirit will fire.		D'un giusto furor.

(*Exit.*)

Scene Fourteen. *Don Ottavio alone.*

DON OTTAVIO

Recitative

Could a gentleman like him	Come mai creder deggio
Be so base and so cruel?	Di si nero delitto
I scarcely can believe it,	Capace un cavaliero!
But I will spare no effort	Ah, di scoprire il vero
Till I find where the truth lies. My heart is torn	Ogni mezzo si cerchi! Io sento in petto

Between the duty of love	E di sposo e d'amico
And the duty of friendship.	Il dover che mi parla:
I must prove her mistaken, or else avenge her!	Disingannarla voglio, o vendicarla.

No. 11. Aria*

My peace and pleasure	[19]	Dalla sua pace
Rest in her keeping.		La mia dipende,
All cares I measure		Quel che a lei piace
But by her weeping.		Vita mi rende,
Trouble that grieves her		Quel che le incresce
Pierces my soul.		Morte mi dà.

Her burdens bearing,	S'ella sospira,
Of pain and sorrow,	Sospiro anch'io;
Her anger sharing,	È mia quell'ira,
Her tears I borrow;	Quel pianto è mio;
When she is absent	È non ho bene,
No joy is whole.	S'ella non l'ha.

(Exit.)

Scene Fifteen. *Leporello alone; then Don Giovanni. / Recitative*

LEPORELLO
(entering)

At all costs I must leave him.	Io deggio ad ogni patto
I cannot serve this madman any longer.	Per sempre abbandonar questo bel matto ...

(Enter Don Giovanni)

And here he comes. Just look at him!	Eccolo qui: guardate
You'd think that he had nothing on his conscience.	Con qual indifferenza se ne viene!

DON GIOVANNI

Oh, my dear Leporello, how are things going?	Oh, Leporello mio, va tutto bene!

LEPORELLO

Things, my dear Don Giovanni, are going badly.	Don Giovannino mio, va tutto male!

DON GIOVANNI

What's that? They're going badly?	Come, va tutto male?

LEPORELLO

I went home, Sir,	Vado a casa,
Just as you gave orders,	Come voi m'ordinaste,
And took those people with me.	Con tutta quella gente.

DON GIOVANNI

Bravo!   Bravo!

LEPORELLO

I talked to them	A forza
Endlessly, I lied to them and charmed them	Di chiacchiere, di vezzi e di bugie,
In the way I've learned so well from you,	Ch'ho imparato sì bene a star con voi,
And they were all delighted.	Cerco d'intrattenerli ...

DON GIOVANNI

Bravo!   Bravo!

LEPORELLO

And I told	Dico
Masetto a thousand things to cheer him	Mille cose a Masetto per placarlo,

---

* This aria was added to the recitative for the 1788 Vienna production, when *'Il mio tesoro'* was cut from Act Two, scene ten.

68

And drive away the jealousy that possessed him.

Per trargli dal pensier la gelosia ...

DON GIOVANNI

Bravo! Well done, upon my honour!

Bravo, bravo, in coscienza mia!

LEPORELLO

I get them drinking ...
Both men and women,
They are all soon half tipsy.
Some are singing, some are fooling,
Others just go on drinking – and at that moment
Who d'you think joined the party?

Faccio che bevano
E gli uomini e le donne,
Son già mezzo ubbriachi:
Altri canta, altri scherza,
Altri seguita a ber ... In sul più bello,
Chi credete che capiti?

DON GIOVANNI

Zerlina!

Zerlina.

LEPORELLO

Bravo! And who came with her?

Bravo! E con lei chi viene?

DON GIOVANNI

Donna Elvira.

Donn'Elvira.

LEPORELLO

Bravo! And said about you ...

Bravo! E disse di voi ...

DON GIOVANNI

Everything bad that her lips had time to utter.

Tutto quel mal che in bocca le venia.

LEPORELLO

Bravo! Well done, upon my honour!

Bravo, bravo, in coscienza mia!

DON GIOVANNI

And then what did you do?

E tu cosa facesti?

LEPORELLO

Nothing.

Tacqui.

DON GIOVANNI

And she?

Ed ella?

LEPORELLO

Just went on shouting.

Seguì a gridar.

DON GIOVANNI

And you?

E tu?

LEPORELLO

When I considered
It was time that she finished, I conducted her
Quite gently from the orchard and, with my usual skill,
I contrived to lock
The gate behind her.
And out there in the road I left her.

Quando mi parve
Che già fosse sfogata, dolcemente
Fuor dell'orto la trassi, e con bell'arte,
Chiusa la porta a chiave,
Io mi cavai,
E sulla via soletta la lasciai.

DON GIOVANNI

Bravo! Bravo! Clever fellow!
You could not have done better. What you have started,
I shall finish myself. These little peasant girls –
What could a man refuse them?
Until the evening comes, I will amuse them.

Bravo! bravo! arcibravo!
L'affar non può andar meglio.
   Incominciasti,
Io saprò terminar: troppo mi premono
Queste contadinotte;
Le voglio divertir finchè vien notte.

Now while the drinking [20]	Fin ch'han dal vino
Stops them from thinking,	Calda la testa,
Feasting and dancing	Una gran festa
We will prepare.	Fa' preparar.
More girls we'll pillage	Se trovi in piazza
Out of the village.	Qualche ragazza,
Search every street	Teco ancor quella
And search every square.	Cerca menar.
Down with formality!	Senza alcun ordine
Mix them together,	La danza sia:
Some minuetting,	Ch'il minuetto,
Some the follia!	Chi la follia,
Clod, cavalier,	Chi l'alemanna
All shall be there.	Farai ballar,
What do I care?	Farai ballar.
For in the meanwhile,	Ed io frattanto,
I shan't be seen while	Dall'altro canto,
I'm cultivating	Con questa e quella
My special flair.	Vo' amoreggiar.
And in the morning,	Ah! la mia lista
You'll be adorning	Doman mattina
Your list with ten more	D'una decina
Names I declare.	Devi aumentar.
You will have ten more,	D'una decina
Ten more I swear.	Devi aumentar.

(*Exeunt.*)

Scene Sixteen. *Don Giovanni's garden; at the back his mansion is illuminated, and there is a pavilion on each side. Peasant men and women are sleeping or sitting on turf seats. Zerlina and Masetto. / Recitative*

ZERLINA

Masetto, listen please, Masetto, listen . . .	Masetto . . . senti un po' . . . Masetto, dico . . .

MASETTO

Keep your hands off.	Non mi toccar.

ZERLINA

But why?	Perchè?

MASETTO

You dare to ask me?	Perchè, mi chiedi?
Faithless girl, d'you think that I could bear the touch	Perfida! Il tatto sopportar dovrei
Of your treacherous hands?	D'una man infedele?

ZERLINA

Oh no, you are too cruel!	Ah, no, taci, crudele!
I've done nothing to deserve such treatment.	Io non merto da te tal trattamento.

MASETTO

Nothing? You'd really pretend that you've done nothing?	Come? Ed hai l'ardimento di scusarti?
You stay alone with a man, leave me for him	Star sola con un uom! abbandonarmi
On this the day of our wedding, and you shame	Il dì delle mie nozze! porre in fronte
A respectable peasant	A un villano d'onore
With the brand of dishonour. Ah, if it were not,	Questa marca d'infamia! Ah, se non fosse,
If it weren't for the scandal, I'd like to . . .	Se non fosse lo scandalo, vorrei . . .

But since I'm not to blame, since it was he Who misled and deceived me, why are you angry? Be calm, my dear, I beg you. He did not touch the tips of my fingers . . . You don't believe me? You're heartless! All right, punish me! Yes, kill me then! Vent All your anger and disgrace me. And then, Masetto darling . . . and then embrace me!	Ma se colpa io non ho! ma se da lui Ingannata rimasi! E poi, che temi? Tranquillati, mia vita: Non mi toccò la punta delle dita. Non me lo credi? Ingrato! Vien qui, sfogati, ammazzami, fa' tutto Di me quel che ti piace: Ma poi, Masetto mio, ma poi fa' pace.

Beat me, beat me, dear Masetto. I am weak and you despise me. Here I stand while you chastise me. Like a lamb I'll bear each blow.	[21]	Batti, batti, o bel Masetto, La tua povera Zerlina: Starò qui come agnellina Le tue botte ad aspettar.
Though you hurt me and abuse me, Tear my hair and scratch my eyes out, Yet I'll kiss the hands that bruise me, For I love you as you know.		Lascerò straziarmi il crine, Lascerò cavarmi gli occhi; E le care tue manine Lieta poi saprò baciar.
Ah, I see now, you're not angry. Let us now make peace, dear lover, All our joy we'll rediscover, Night and day our love shall grow.	[22]	Ah, lo vedo, non hai core! Pace, pace, o vita mia! In contenti ed allegria Notte e di vogliam passar.

Recitative

Look at that, the little witch! She knows how to get round me. It just shows That we men are weak and stupid.	Guarda un po' come seppe Questa strega sedurmi! Siamo pure I deboli di testa!

See everything is ready for a great banquet.	Sia preparato tutto a una gran festa.

Ah, Masetto, Masetto, did you hear that? It's the voice of his lordship!	Ah, Masetto, Masetto, odi la voce Del monsù cavaliero!

And what of that?	Ebben, che c'è?

He's coming.	Verrà.

Well, let him come then.	Lascia che venga.

Ah, if I only Could find a place to hide.	Ah! se vi fosse Un buco da fuggir!

Why are you frightened? And why all this confusion? . . . Ah! I see now, I see, you little wanton, You're afraid I'll discover What passed between you and your noble lover!	Di cosa temi? Perchè diventi pallida? . . . Ah! capisco, Capisco, bricconcella: Hai timor ch'io comprenda Com'è tra voi passata la faccenda.

Quickly, quickly! While he's coming, [23]
I must find a place to hide here.
See this arbour! Just inside here
I'll conceal myself and wait.

Presto, presto . . . pria ch'ei venga,
Por mi vo' da qualche lato . . .
C'è una nicchia . . . qui celato
Cheto, cheto mi vo' star.

ZERLINA

Listen, listen! Why this hiding?
Your jealousy, Masetto, blinds you!
Do consider, if he finds you,
Then his fury will be great.

Senti . . . senti . . . dove vai?
Ah, non t'asconder, o Masetto!
Se ti trova, poveretto,
Tu non sai quel che può far.

MASETTO

I don't fear your precious master.

Faccia, dica quel che vuole.

ZERLINA
(aside)

He will bring us to disaster.

Ah, non giovan le parole . . .

MASETTO

I shall hear what both are saying.

Parla forte, e qui t'arresta.

ZERLINA
(aside)

It is mad, this game he's playing!
His behaviour will destroy us,
Why must he exaggerate?

Che capriccio ha nella testa!
Quell'ingrato, quel crudele
Oggi vuol precipitar.

MASETTO
(aside)

Soon I'll know if she is faithful,
I will learn to love or hate.

Capirò se m'è fedele,
E in qual modo andò l'affar.

(He goes into a pavilion.)

Scene Seventeen. *Zerlina, Don Giovanni, servants, peasant men and women.*

DON GIOVANNI
(to the peasants)

Now good fellows do your duty.
Pleasure is today's employment:
Look to everyone's enjoyment,
Spread contentment and goodwill.

Su, svegliatevi, da bravi!
Su, coraggio, o buona gente:
Vogliam stare allegramente,
Vogliam ridere e scherzar.

(to the servants)

To the ballroom lead them all,
And see that no-one there is lonely.
Give them food and wine in plenty.
Let them dance and drink their fill.

Alla stanza della danza
Conducete tutti quanti,
Ed a tutti in abbondanza
Gran rinfreschi fate dar.

CHORUS OF SERVANTS

Now prepare for more enjoyment.
There'll be dancing, there'll be laughter,
And a splendid supper after,
Spreading friendship and goodwill.

Su, svegliatevi, da bravi!
Su, coraggio, o buona gente:
Vogliam stare allegramente,
Vogliam ridere e scherzar.

(Exeunt servants and peasants.)

Scene Eighteen. *Zerlina, Don Giovanni; Masetto in the pavilion.*

ZERLINA
(aside)

There's a chance he won't detect me
If I hide behind this corner.

Tra quest'arbori celata
Si può dar che non mi veda.

(She tries to hide.)

DON GIOVANNI

Sweet Zerlina, you'd reject me.	Zerlinetta mia garbata,
I can see you, don't take fright.	T'ho già visto, non scappar.

(He catches her.)

ZERLINA

Oh, my lord, I cannot stay here!	Ah! lasciatemi andar via . . .

DON GIOVANNI

Hear the words that I must say, dear.	No, no; resta, gioia mia!

ZERLINA

Have some pity, I implore you . . .	Se pietade avete in core . . .

DON GIOVANNI

Yes, my darling, I adore you.	Si, ben mio, son tutto amore . . .
Come with me inside that arbour:	Vieni un poco in questo loco:
Love and Fortune both invite.	Fortunata io ti vo' far.

ZERLINA
(aside)

If my bridegroom finds us now,	Ah, s'ei vede il sposo mio,
I fear there'll be a dreadful fight.	So ben io quel che può far.

(Don Giovanni opens the door to the pavilion and, seeing Masetto, shows his surprise.)

DON GIOVANNI

Masetto?	Masetto!

MASETTO

Yes, Masetto.	Si, Masetto.

DON GIOVANNI
(somewhat embarrassed)

But why in hiding there?	E chiuso là, perchè?

(regaining his confidence)

Deserting poor Zerlina!	La bella tua Zerlina
If you had only seen her.	Non può, la poverina,
She needs your loving care.	Più star senza di te.

MASETTO
(with slight irony)

Your words, my lord, I'll treasure.	Capisco: si, signore.

DON GIOVANNI
(to Zerlina)

Now let us think of pleasure,	Adesso fate core,
Only pleasure!	Fate core!
The dance is just beginning,	I suonatori udite:
We'll go and take our share.	Venite omai con me.

MASETTO AND ZERLINA

Yes, yes, let's think of pleasure.	Si, si, facciamo core,
The others all are dancing,	Ed a ballar con gli altri
We'll go and take our share.	Andiamo tutti e tre.

(Exeunt.)

Scene Nineteen. *Donna Anna, Donna Elvira, Don Ottavio, masked; then Don Giovanni and Leporello at the window.*

DONNA ELVIRA
(entering with Donna Anna and Don Ottavio)

Now summon all your courage,	[24] Bisogna aver coraggio,
The task is clear before us.	O cari amici miei,
Unmask the cruel traitor,	E i suoi misfatti rei
And all his sins reveal.	Scoprir potremo allor.

Dear friend, your words are timely,
Our purpose shall not alter!
(to Donna Anna)
We will not fail or falter,
Whatever doubts we feel!

L'amica dice bene:
Coraggio aver conviene.
(to Donna Anna)
Discaccia, o vita mia,
L'affanno ed il timor.

DONNA ANNA

With terror I am shaking –
A fatal step we're taking:
I fear for you, my dearest,
In this hour's dread ordeal.

Il passo è periglioso,
Può nascer qualche imbroglio;
Temo pel caro sposo
E per noi temo ancor.

LEPORELLO
(coming out onto the balcony of the mansion with Don Giovanni) [25]

My lord, see through the garden
Three maskers are advancing.

Signor, guardate un poco
Che maschere galanti!

DON GIOVANNI

Ask them to join the dancing,
Whoever they may be.

Falle passar avanti,
Di' che ci fanno onor.

(He goes back inside.)

DONNA ANNA, DONNA ELVIRA AND DON OTTAVIO
(aside)

That voice and manner surely
Disclose the man we're seeking.

Al volto ed alla voce
Si scopre il traditor.

LEPORELLO

Psst! Psst! You masqueraders there!
Psst! Psst!

Zi, zi! Signore maschere!
Zi, zi . . .

DONNA ANNA AND DONNA ELVIRA
(sottovoce to Don Ottavio)

Now you must answer!

Via, rispondete.

LEPORELLO

Psst! Psst! You masqueraders there!

Zi, zi, Signore maschere!

DON OTTAVIO
(to Leporello)

Why are you calling?

Cosa chiedete?

LEPORELLO

To dance my lord invites you
So please come in all three.

Al ballo, se vi piace,
V'invita il mio signor.

DON OTTAVIO
(to Leporello)

Pray thank him for this honour.
(to Donna Anna and Donna Elvira)
Come, friends, we'll dance a measure.

Grazie di tanto onore.
(to Donna Anna and Donna Elvira)
Andiam, compagne belle.

LEPORELLO
(aside)

Your friends will give him pleasure
As you will shortly see.

L'amico anche su quelle
Prova farà d'amor.

(He goes back inside and shuts the balcony window.)

DONNA ANNA AND DON OTTAVIO

May Heaven protect and bless now [26]
The justice of our cause.

Protegga il giusto cielo
Il zelo del mio cor.

DONNA ELVIRA

May Heaven at last avenge now
Love and its flouted laws.

Vendichi il giusto cielo
Il mio traditor amor.

(Exeunt.)

Scene Twenty. *A room lighted and prepared for a great ball. Don Giovanni, Leporello, Zerlina, Masetto, peasant men and women, musicians, servants with refreshments. Don Giovanni shows the peasant women to their seats and Leporello the men; they have just finished a dance.*

DON GIOVANNI

Ladies, rest for a moment, I pray you.　　　Riposate, vezzose ragazze!

LEPORELLO

You, young men, time for drinking, what say you?　　　Rinfrescatevi, bei giovinotti!

DON GIOVANNI AND LEPORELLO

When you've all had some rest and refreshment,　　　Tornerete a far presto le pazze,
You can go back to dancing again.　　　Tornerete a scherzar e ballar.

(Refreshments are brought.)

DON GIOVANNI

Coffee here.　　　Ehi, caffè!

LEPORELLO

Hot chocolate.　　　Cioccolata!

MASETTO
(sottovoce to Zerlina)

Now, Zerlina, be careful.　　　Ah, Zerlina: giudizio!

DON GIOVANNI

The ices!　　　Sorbetti!

LEPORELLO

Sugared almonds!　　　Confetti!

ZERLINA AND MASETTO
(aside)

What begins in sweet innocent pleasure　　　Troppo dolce comincia la scena:
Ends in bitter repentance and pain.　　　In amaro potria terminar.

DON GIOVANNI
(caressing Zerlina)

You look charming, my lovely Zerlina!　　　Sei pur vaga, brillante Zerlina!

ZERLINA
(to Don Giovanni)

You're too kind ...　　　Sua bontà ...

MASETTO
(looking and trembling with rage; aside)

How his flattery delights her.　　　La briccona fa festa.

LEPORELLO
(imitating his master with the other girls)

You look charming, Giannotta, Sandrina!　　　Sei pur cara, Giannotta, Sandrina!

MASETTO
(aside, watching Don Giovanni)

Just you touch her and you'll have to fight, Sir.　　　Tocca pur, che ti cada la testa!

ZERLINA
(aside)

Poor Masetto is getting so angry　　　Quel Masetto mi par stralunato:
There'll be trouble quite soon, that is plain.　　　Brutto brutto si fa quest'affar.

75

DON GIOVANNI AND LEPORELLO
(aside)

Poor Masetto is getting so angry,
His behaviour we'll have to restrain.

Quel Masetto mi par stralunato;
Qui bisogna cervello adoprar.

MASETTO
(aside, in Zerlina's direction)

O you wanton, you'll drive me insane.

Ah, briccona, mi vuoi disperar!

Scene Twenty-one. *Don Giovanni, Leporello, Zerlina, Masetto, peasant men and women, musicians, servants, Donna Anna, Donna Elvira and Don Ottavio. Enter Donna Anna, Donna Elvira and Don Ottavio, masked.*

LEPORELLO

Pray step this way, and welcome,
O charming masqueraders!

Venite pur avanti,
Vezzose mascherette!

DON GIOVANNI

To everyone a welcome,
Long live our liberty!

È aperto a tutti quanti:
Viva la libertà!

DONNA ANNA, DONNA ELVIRA AND DON OTTAVIO

We thank you for this greeting
So generous and free.

Siam grati a tanti segni
Di generosità!

DONNA ANNA, DONNA ELVIRA, DON OTTAVIO, DON GIOVANNI AND LEPORELLO

Long live our liberty!

Viva la libertà!

DON GIOVANNI
(to the musicians)

Now let us have more music.

Ricominciate il suono.

(to Leporello, who is to organise the dance)

Find everyone a partner.

Tu accoppia i ballerini.

LEPORELLO

Come, all must join the dancing.

Da bravi, via, ballate.

(They dance. Don Ottavio dances a minuet with Donna Anna.)

DONNA ELVIRA
(sottovoce to Donna Anna)

There is the girl I spoke of.

Quella è la contadina.

DONNA ANNA
(sottovoce to Don Ottavio)

I tremble!

Io moro!

DON OTTAVIO
(sottovoce to Donna Anna)

Still dissemble.

Simulate.

DON GIOVANNI AND LEPORELLO

All happy as could be!

Va bene, in verità!

MASETTO
(sarcastically)

All happy! All happy!
All happy as could be!

Va bene, va bene,
Va bene, in verità!

DON GIOVANNI
(sottovoce to Leporello)

Look after our Masetto.

A bada tien Masetto.

LEPORELLO
(to Masetto)

Masetto, aren't you dancing?
Just look at all the rest, Masetto!
They're dancing, so must we.

Non balli, poveretto?
Vien qua, Masetto caro:
Facciam quel ch'altri fa.

DON GIOVANNI
(to Zerlina)

Now I shall be your partner, Zerlina,	Il tuo compagno io sono,
Zerlina, come with me!	Zerlina, vien pur qua!

(He begins to dance a contredanse with Zerlina.)

MASETTO

I will not dance, I tell you!	No, no, ballar non voglio.

LEPORELLO

Come, dance, or I'll compel you.	Eh, balla, amico mio!

MASETTO

No.	No!

LEPORELLO

Yes.	Sì!
My dear Masetto, dance now.	Caro Masetto, balla!
Just do like all the others,	Eh balla, amico mio,
They're dancing, so shall we.	Facciam quel ch'altri fa.

DONNA ANNA
(sottovoce to Donna Elvira)

I can endure no longer!	Resister non poss'io!

DONNA ELVIRA AND DON OTTAVIO
(to Donna Anna)

Still brave and constant be!	Fingete, per pietà!

(Leporello dances the Deutscher with Masetto.)

DON GIOVANNI
(to Zerlina)

Come dear, you need not fear me,	Vieni con me, mia vita ...
Come dear, come dear ...	Vieni, vieni ...

(He leads Zerlina dancing towards a door, and almost pushes her through.)

MASETTO
(to Leporello)

Let me go! ... Ah, no! ... Zerlina!	Lasciami ... Ah ... no ... Zerlina!

ZERLINA

Let go, Sir! You've deceived me!	Oh, numi! son tradita! ...

(Masetto frees himself from Leporello and goes after Zerlina.)

LEPORELLO
(aside)

This time it's a disaster!	Qui nasce una ruina.

(He hurries after Don Giovanni.)

DONNA ANNA, DONNA ELVIRA AND DON OTTAVIO

The wicked man approaches	L'iniquo da se stesso
The trap he cannot see!	Nel laccio se ne va.

ZERLINA
(She screams. Then off-stage, she shrieks and a confused noise of footsteps is heard)

Friends! ... Oh, help me! ... Come and save me!	Gente! ... Aiuto! ...Aiuto, gente!

DONNA ANNA, DONNA ELVIRA AND DON OTTAVIO

Quickly, quickly, run and save her!	Soccorriamo l'innocente!

(The musicians and others leave in confusion.)

MASETTO

Ah, Zerlina! ...	Ah, Zerlina! ...

ZERLINA
(*within*)

Foul seducer! Scellerato!

(*Her screams and the noise of running are now heard from the other side.*)

DONNA ANNA, DONNA ELVIRA AND DON OTTAVIO

Now she calls from that direction ...   Ora grida da quel lato ...
Now we'll have to force an entrance.   Ah! gettiamo giù la porta ...

(*They force the door.*)

ZERLINA
(*coming out from a different side*)

Come and rescue me, I'm dying!   Soccorretemi, son morta! ...

DONNA ANNA, DONNA ELVIRA, DON OTTAVIO AND MASETTO

We are coming to protect you.   Siam qui noi per tua difesa.

DON GIOVANNI
(*He enters dragging Leporello by the arm, but pretending to be unable to unsheathe his sword to strike him. To Zerlina.*)

Here's the scoundrel who attacked you!   Ecco il birbo che t'ha offesa,
I will see he pays the price.   Ma da me la pena avrà.

(*to Leporello*)

You shall die, wretch.   Mori, iniquo!

LEPORELLO

Oh, let me go, Sir!   Ah! cosa fate? ...

DON GIOVANNI

Die, I tell you!   Mori, dico!

DON OTTAVIO
(*drawing a pistol on Don Giovanni*)

All your lies and tricks we know, Sir!   Nol sperate, nol sperate!

DONNA ANNA, DONNA ELVIRA AND DON OTTAVIO
(*removing their masks*)

This deception will not save you.   L'empio crede con tal frode
You are guilty, you alone.   Di nasconder l'empietà.

DON GIOVANNI
(*recognizing them*)

Donn'Elvira!   Donn'Elvira!

DONNA ELVIRA

Yes, you villain!   Si, malvaggio!

DON GIOVANNI

Don Ottavio?   Don Ottavio!

DON OTTAVIO

As you see, Sir.   Si, signore!

DON GIOVANNI
(*to Donna Anna*)

Ah, believe me!   Ah! credete ...

DONNA ANNA, DONNA ELVIRA, ZERLINA, DON OTTAVIO AND MASETTO

Vile deceiver!   Traditore! Traditore!

ZERLINA

All your evil deeds are known!   Tutto, tutto già si sa.

All your evil deeds are known!	Tutto, tutto già si sa.
Evil! Evil! Evil!	Tutto! tutto! tutto!
Tremble, tremble, foul seducer!	Trema, trema scellerato!
Your debauchery, pernicious,	Saprà tosto il mondo intero
Every deed corrupt and vicious,	Il misfatto orrendo e nero,
To the world we shall display.	La tua fiera credeltà.
See the lightning flash of vengeance,	Odi il tuon della vendetta
Angry Heaven parts asunder,	Che ti fischia intorno intorno:
And at last its wrath will thunder	Sul tuo capo, in questo giorno,
On your guilty head today!	Il suo fulmine cadrà.

DON GIOVANNI AND LEPORELLO

Dreadful dangers gather round{ me, / him,

Paralysing{ my / his invention,

And this sudden intervention

Throws{ my / his plans in disarray.

But{ my / his courage shall not fail{ me, / him,

Though the powers of Hell assail { me! / him!

Let the Day of Judgment threaten,

Faithful to{ myself I'll / himself he'll stay!

È confusa la { mia / sua testa,

Non { so / sa più quel ch'{ io mi / ei si faccia,

E un'orribile tempesta

Minacciando, oddio! { mi / lo va!

Ma non manca in{ me / lui coraggio:

Non { mi perdo / si perde o { mi confondo. / si confonde.

Se cadesse ancora il mondo

Nulla mai temer{ mi / lo fa!

End of the First Act

The gardens of Don Giovanni's palace designed by Franco Zeffirelli for his 1962 Covent Garden production.

Act Two

Scene One. *A street; on one side is Donna Elvira's house, with a balcony. Don Giovanni and Leporello. / No. 15. Duet*

DON GIOVANNI

I don't believe you. It's simply bluff.   [27] Eh, via buffone, non mi seccar!

LEPORELLO

I mean to leave you. I've had enough!   No, no, padrone, non vo' restar!

DON GIOVANNI

You're only playing . . .   Sentimi, amico . . .

LEPORELLO

            No, I'm not staying.   Vo' andar, vi dico.

DON GIOVANNI

But can you give me some explanation?   Ma che ti ho fatto, che vuoi lasciarmi?

LEPORELLO

Merely attempted assassination.   Oh, niente affatto: quasi ammazzarmi!

DON GIOVANNI

Don't be so silly; that was in fun.   Va', che sei matto; fu per burlar.

LEPORELLO

The fun is over, and I have done.   Ed io non burlo, ma voglio andar.

(He starts to leave, but Don Giovanni calls him back.)

Recitative

DON GIOVANNI

Leporello.   Leporello.

LEPORELLO

    I'm listening.   Signore.

DON GIOVANNI

Come here, we'll make a treaty. Take this!   Vien qui, facciamo pace. Prendi . . .

LEPORELLO

What?   Cosa?

DON GIOVANNI
(giving him some money)

Four gold pieces.   Quattro doppie.

LEPORELLO

        Oh . . . In that case,   Oh! sentite:
Just for this once   Per questa volta
I'll agree to an arrangement.   La cerimonia accetto.
But this is an exception. I am not   Ma non vi ci avvezzate: non credete
The sort of man to be seduced,   Di sedurre i miei pari,
With offers of money, as if I were a woman.   Come le donne, a forza di danari.

DON GIOVANNI

We'll say no more of that. Are you   Non parliam più di ciò. Ti basta
    the sort of man   l'animo
To carry out my wishes?   Di far quel ch'io ti dico?

LEPORELLO

If you will give up women.   Purchè lasciam le donne.

80

I, give up women? Madman!
I, give up women! You know very well
That I need women more than food and drink
Or the air that I breath!

Lasciar le donne! Pazzo!
Lasciar le donne? Sai ch'elle per me
Son necessarie più del pan che mangio,
Più dell'aria che spiro!

LEPORELLO

But then how can you
Have the heart to desert them?

E avete core
D'ingannarle poi tutte?

DON GIOVANNI

Because I love them.
To be faithful to one woman
Means neglecting the others.
My feelings are so
Wide-ranging and extensive,
I'd have all the women share them.
But they, alas, can't grasp this fine conception;
My generous good nature they call deception.

È tutto amore:
Chi a una sola è fedele
Verso l'altre è crudele.
Io, che in me sento
Sì esteso sentimento,
Vo' bene a tutte quante.
Le donne, poi che calcolar non sanno,
Il mio buon natural chiamano inganno.

LEPORELLO

I never saw a nature
Of such splendid proportions, or half so generous.
Well then, what do you want?

Non ho veduto mai
Naturale più vasto e più benigno.
Orsù, cosa vorreste?

DON GIOVANNI

Listen! Have you observed the girl who waits
On Donn'Elvira?

Odi: vedesti tu la cameriera
Di Donn'Elvira?

LEPORELLO

Not yet.

Io no.

DON GIOVANNI

Then you're unlucky.
She's a thing of great beauty,
My dear Leporello! I'll try my fortune
With this lady-in-waiting. And my intention,
Since evening is upon us,
Is to disguise myself when I approach her.
So lend me now at once your hat and cloak, Sir.

Non hai veduto
Qualche cosa di bello,
Caro il mio Leporello! Ora io con lei
Vo' tentar la mia sorte; ed ho pensato,
Giacchè siam verso sera,
Per aguzzarle meglio l'appetito,
Di presentarmi a lei col tuo vestito.

LEPORELLO

But why should you not meet her
In the ones you are wearing?

E perchè non potreste
Presentarvi col vostro?

DON GIOVANNI

It's most unfortunate,
But women of her station
Don't seem to trust the gentry.

Han poco credito
Con gente di tal rango
Gli abiti signorili.

(He takes off his own cloak.)

Off with them. Quickly.

Sbrigati, via!

LEPORELLO

My lord, my own position ...

Signor ... per più ragioni ...

DON GIOVANNI
(angrily)

That's quite enough! I'll have no opposition.

Finiscila! Non soffro opposizioni.

(They exchange cloaks.)

Scene Two. *Don Giovanni, Leporello and Donna Elvira on the balcony. Night falls gradually.* / *No. 16. Trio*

DONNA ELVIRA

My suffering heart be silent!　　[28]　Ah, taci, ingiusto core,
Oh still this hopeless yearning.　　　　Non palpitarmi in seno:
He's faithless, as he is violent;　　　　È un empio, è un traditore.
To pity him were sin.　　　　　　　　È colpa aver pietà.

LEPORELLO
(*sottovoce*)

Hush that is Donn'Elvira;　　　　Zitto . . . di Donn'Elvira,
My lord, can you not hear her?　　Signor, la voce io sento.

DON GIOVANNI
(*sottovoce*)

This chance must not be wasted;　　Cogliere io vo' il momento.
Stand there and I'll begin.　　　　Tu fermati un po' là.
　　　　(*He stands behind Leporello and addresses Donna Elvira.*)
Elvira, I adore you.　　　　　　　Elvira, idolo mio! . . .

DONNA ELVIRA

Is that the cruel traitor?　　　　Non è costui l'ingrato?

DON GIOVANNI

Yes, here he stands before you,　　Sì, mia vita, son io;
And begs you to forgive.　　　　　E chiedo carità.

DONNA ELVIRA
(*aside*)

What strange familiar feeling!　　Numi, che strano affetto
My heart again is stealing.　　　Mi si risveglia in petto!

LEPORELLO
(*aside*)

Watch now this foolish woman;　　State a veder la pazza,
Once more she will believe.　　　Che ancor gli crederà.

DON GIOVANNI

Come down, my love, my fair one,　　Discendi, o gioia bella!
Come down to bless and spare one　　Vedrai che tu sei quella
Who offers true repentance:　　　　Che adora l'alma mia:
Without you he cannot live.　　　　Pentito io sono già.

DONNA ELVIRA

Too often I have trusted you!　　No, non ti credo, o barbaro!

DON GIOVANNI
(*affecting anguish*)

Believe in me, or I die here!　　Ah, credimi, o m'uccido!

LEPORELLO
(*sottovoce to Don Giovanni*)

Soon I shall burst out laughing.　　Se seguitate, io rido.

DON GIOVANNI

Take now the heart I give.　　　Idolo mio, vien qua.

DONNA ELVIRA
(*aside*)

Can this be true repenting?　　Dei, che cimento è questo?
I feel my heart relenting.　　Non so s'io vado o resto . . .
Defend and guide, oh Heaven!　　Ah! proteggete voi
My all too trusting heart.　　La mia credulità.

DON GIOVANNI
(aside)

Soon she will be consenting.	Spero che cada presto.
She thinks I am repenting.	Che bel colpetto è questo!
There's no-one with my talent	Più fertile talento
For acting such a part.	Del mio, no, non si dà.

LEPORELLO
(aside)

Those lying lips already	Già quel mendace labbro
Have once again misled her.	Torna a sedur costei:
Defend and guide her, oh Heaven,	Deh! proteggete, o Dei,
And her too trusting heart.	La sua credulità.

(Donna Elvira leaves the balcony.)

Recitative

DON GIOVANNI
(gaily)

Well, what d'you say to that?	Amico, che ti par?

LEPORELLO

To me it's quite clear,	Mi par che abbiate
Your heart is made of stone.	Un'anima di bronzo.

DON GIOVANNI

And your head is made of bone. Now pay attention:	Va' là, che se' il gran gonzo! Ascolta bene:
When she comes out to meet me,	Quando costei qui viene,
Run forward and embrace her.	Tu corri ad abbracciarla:
Make a bit of a fuss of her,	Falle quattro carezze,
Imitate my way of speaking and then contrive	Fingi la voce mia; poi con bell'arte
To take her with you a good long way from this place.	Cerca teco condurla in altra parte.

LEPORELLO

But your lordship . . .	Ma signore . . .

DON GIOVANNI

No more arguing.	Non più repliche!

LEPORELLO

But suppose she discovers?	E se poi mi conosce?

DON GIOVANNI
(holding a pistol to Leporello's nose)

She'll never find out if you don't help her.	Non ti conoscerà, se tu non vuoi.
Quiet. She's coming now. Hey, be clever!	Zitto: ell'apre. Ehi, giudizio!

(He goes upstage.)

Scene Three. *Don Giovanni, Leporello and Donna Elvira.*

DONNA ELVIRA

See, I am here.	Eccomi a voi.

DON GIOVANNI
(withdrawing upstage; aside)

Let's see how he gets on.	Veggiamo che farà.

LEPORELLO
(aside)

What a fine mess.	Che imbroglio!

DONNA ELVIRA
(to Leporello, mistaking him for Don Giovanni)

Can I really believe my tears and suffering
Subdued that cold heart? Have you repented,
Beloved Don Giovanni? And to your duty
And love you're now returning?

Dunque, creder potrò che i pianti miei
Abbian vinto quel cor? Dunque, pentito
L'amato Don Giovanni al suo dovere
E all'amor mio ritorna? ...

LEPORELLO
(changing his voice)

Yes, my sweetest!

Si, carina!

DONNA ELVIRA

Oh, cruel one! If you only knew
How many tears and how many
Sighs you have cost me! ...

Crudele! Se sapeste
Quante lagrime e quanti
Sospir voi mi costate! ...

LEPORELLO

I, my beloved?

Io, vita mia?

DONNA ELVIRA

Yes, you.

Voi.

LEPORELLO

Poor Elvira! I am so very sorry.

Poverina! Quanto mi dispiace!

DONNA ELVIRA

You won't leave me again?

Mi fuggirete più?

LEPORELLO

No, pretty creature.

No, muso bello.

DONN ELVIRA

You'll be my own for ever?

Sarete sempre mio?

LEPORELLO

Ever.

Sempre.

DONNA ELVIRA

My dearest one!

Carissimo!

LEPORELLO

My dearest one!
(aside)
This game is not unpleasant.

Carissima!

La burla mi dà gusto.

DONNA ELVIRA

My adored one!

Mio tesoro!

LEPORELLO

My Venus!

Mia Venere!

DONNA ELVIRA

All my being's on fire for you.

Son per voi tutto fuoco.

LEPORELLO

I've turned to ashes.

Io tutto cenere.

DON GIOVANNI
(aside)

He's warming to it nicely.

Il birbo si riscalda.

DONNA ELVIRA

And you will not deceive me?

E non m'ingannerete?

LEPORELLO

Why, of course not!

No, sicuro.

DONNA ELVIRA

You swear it?   Giuratemi.

LEPORELLO

I swear it by this hand,   Lo giuro a questa man,
Which I cover with my kisses. And by those   Che bacio con trasporto, e a quei bei
    dear eyes ...   lumi ...

DON GIOVANNI
(pretending to kill someone with his sword)

Ay! ay! ay! That's got you!   Ih! eh! ah! ih! Sei morto!

DONNA ELVIRA AND LEPORELLO

Oh Heavens!   Oh, Numi!

(They flee.)

DON GIOVANNI
(laughing)

Ay, ay, ay, ay! My luck at last   Ih, eh, ih, eh, ah, ih! Par che la sorte
It seems is turning. That's better.   Mi secondi. Veggiamo:
Yes, there is her window. Now for the   Le finestre son queste. Ora cantiamo.
    canzonetta!

No. 17. Canzonetta

Oh, look from out thy window, my   [29]   Deh, vieni alla finestra, o mio tesoro!
    dearest treasure,
And let thine eyes console my tears and   Deh, vieni a consolar il pianto mio:
    sighing.
No longer now deny some hope of   Se neghi a me di dar qualche ristoro,
    pleasure,
Or those same eyes I love shall see me   Davanti agli occhi tuoi morir vogl'io.
    dying.

Thy lips to me are sweeter far than   Tu ch'hai la bocca dolce più che il
    honey,   miele,
Sweeter yet is the kindness in thy heart   Tu che il zucchero porti in mezzo il
    glowing.   core,
If that dear heart grow cold, thou hast   Non esser, gioia mia, con me crudele:
    undone me!
Life to thy lover give, one glance   Lasciati almen veder, mio bell'amore!
    bestowing.

Scene Four. *Don Giovanni, Masetto and armed peasants. / Recitative*

DON GIOVANNI

There's someone at the window. Is it she?   V'è gente alla finestra: sarà dessa.
Psst! Psst!   Zi, zi.

MASETTO
(entering with the peasants)

We won't give up yet. I have a feeling   Non ci stanchiamo: il cor mi dice
That he's not far away.   Che trovarlo dobbiam.

DON GIOVANNI
(aside)

Who is that speaking?   Qualcuno parla.

MASETTO

Stop all of you! I think   Fermatevi: mi pare
I can hear somebody moving.   Che alcuno qui si muova.

DON GIOVANNI
(aside)

I am sure that's Masetto.   Se non fallo è Masetto.

MASETTO
(aloud)

Who goes there?   Chi va là?

85

(to the peasants)

No-one answers.　　　　　　　　　　　　　　　　Non risponde.
Have all your weapons ready.　　　　　　　　Animo: schioppo al muso!
　　　　　　　　　　　　　　　　(louder)
Who goes there?　　　　　　　　　　　　　　　Chi va là?

DON GIOVANNI
(aside)

He's with others.　　　　　　　　　　　　　Non è solo:
I must be careful.　　　　　　　　　　　　　Ci vuol giudizio.
　　　　　(He tries to imitate Leporello's voice.)
A friend . . .　　　　　　　　　　　　　　　　Amici . . .
　　　　　　　　　　　(aside)
He must not recognize me.　　　　　　　　　Non mi voglio scoprir.
　　　　　　　　　(as before)
Is that Masetto?　　　　　　　　　　　　　　　Sei tu, Masetto?

MASETTO
(angrily)

Yes, I'm Masetto. And you?　　　　　　　Appunto quello. E tu?

DON GIOVANNI

Do you not know me? The servant　　　Non mi conosci? Il servo
Of Don Giovanni.　　　　　　　　　　　　　Son io di Don Giovanni.

MASETTO

Leporello!　　　　　　　　　　　　　　　　　Leporello!
Servant of that worthless highborn ruffian?　　Servo di quell'indigno cavaliere!

DON GIOVANNI

Quite right. Of that vile scoundrel . . .　　Certo: di quel briccone . . .

MASETTO

Of that man without honour. And　　Di quell'uom senza onore! Ah, dimmi un
you'll be able　　　　　　　　　　　　　　poco
To tell us where to find him:　　　　　Dove possiam trovarlo:
We're looking for him so that we can kill　　Lo cerco con costor per trucidarlo.
him.

DON GIOVANNI
(aside)

Is that all?　　　　　　　　　　　　　　　Bagattelle!
　　　　　　　　　(aloud)
You're doing well, Masetto,　　　　　　Bravissimo, Masetto!
And I would like to join you　　　　　Anch'io con voi m'unisco
To pay off some old scores against my　　Per fargliela a quel birbo di padrone.
master.
Follow my plan and we shall catch him　　Or senti un po' qual è la mia intenzione.
faster.

No. 18. Aria

(pointing to the right)
Let half your men go over there,　　[30]　Metà di voi qua vadano,
　　　　　　　(pointing to the left)
And half the other way.　　　　　　　E gli altri vadan là,
And softly, seek him everywhere.　　E pian pianin lo cerchino:
He can't be far away.　　　　　　　　Lontan non fia di qua.

If some of you discover　　　　　　　Se un uom e una ragazza
A woman and her lover,　　　　　　　Passeggian per la piazza;
Or hear beneath a window　　　　　　Se sotto a una finestra
A serenader like him,　　　　　　　　Fare all'amor sentite,
Then go for him and strike him.　　Ferite pur, ferite:
It's sure to be my lord.　　　　　　　Il mio padron sarà!

You'll know him by his bearing,　　In testa egli ha un cappello
His hat with great white feathers,　　Con candidi pennacchini;
The long cloak he is wearing,　　　Addosso un gran mantello,
His sharp and deadly sword.　　　　E spada al fianco egli ha.

Each man to his position!	Andate, fate presto!

(Exeunt peasants. To Masetto)

But you shall come with me.	Tu sol verrai con me.
We have a separate mission,	Noi far dobbiamo il resto;
As you will shortly see.	E già vedrai cos'è.

(Exit, taking Masetto with him.)

Scene Five. *Don Giovanni and Masetto. / Recitative*

DON GIOVANNI
(Coming back on-stage, leading Masetto by the hand.)

Quiet now . . . while I listen. Good, I hear nothing.	Zitto . . . Lascia ch'io senta . . . Ottimamente.
So we must really kill the man?	Dunque, dobbiam ucciderlo.

MASETTO

We must.	Sicuro.

DON GIOVANNI

It wouldn't be enough to break a few bones,	E non ti basteria rompergli l'ossa,
And beat his shoulders to pulp?	Fracassargli le spalle . . .

MASETTO

No, no, I want to kill him	No, no: voglio ammazzarlo,
And tear him into pieces.	Vo' farlo in cento brani.

DON GIOVANNI

You've got good weapons?	Hai buone armi?

MASETTO

I should say so!	Cospetto!
See here, I have this musket	Ho pria questo moschetto
And then I have this pistol.	E poi questa pistola.

(He gives the musket and pistol to Don Giovanni.)

DON GIOVANNI

Is that all?	E poi?

MASETTO

Do I need more?	Non basta?

DON GIOVANNI

No, these are plenty. Let's try them.	Oh, basta, certo! Or prendi:

(He beats Masetto with the flat of his sword.)

That's for your little pistol . . .	Questa per la pistola . . .
And that's for your great big musket.	Questa per il moschetto . . .

MASETTO

Oh, oh, oh, help! Oh, help!	Ahi! ahi! . . . soccorso! Ahi! ahi!

DON GIOVANNI
(threatening him with the guns)

Hush or I'll kill you!	Taci, o sei morto!
That's for wanting to tear him,	Questi per l'ammazzarlo,
And that's for wanting to kill him.	Questi per farlo in brani.
You coarse and stupid brute, you stinking vermin!	Villano, mascalzon, ceffo da cani!

(Exit.)

Scene Six. *Masetto; then Zerlina with a lantern.*

MASETTO
(crying out loud)

Oh, oh, my head is broken!	Ahi! ahi! la testa mia!
Oh, oh, my shoulders, my ribs!	Ahi! ahi! le spalle . . . e il petto!

ZERLINA
(entering)

I'm sure that I heard	Di sentire mi parve
The voice of my Masetto.	La voce di Masetto.

MASETTO

Oh God! Zerlina!	Oddio! Zerlina . . .
My dear Zerlina, oh help me!	Zerlina mia, soccorso!

ZERLINA

What has happened?	Cosa è stato?

MASETTO

That villain, that vicious blackguard	L'iniquo, il scellerato
Has broken me in pieces.	Mi ruppe l'ossa e i nervi.

ZERLINA

Tell me for Heaven's sake! Who?	Oh, poveretta me! Chi?

MASETTO

Leporello!	Leporello!
Or else some devil who looked just like him.	O qualche diavol che somiglia a lui.

ZERLINA

The brute! Did I not tell you	Crudel! Non tel diss'io
That your stupid and jealous behaviour	Che con questa tua pazza gelosia
Would in the end only get you into trouble?	Ti ridurresti a qualche brutto passo?
Where does it hurt you?	Dove ti duole?

MASETTO

Here.	Qui.

ZERLINA

And where else?	E poi?

MASETTO

Here, and also here.	Qui . . . e ancora qui . . .

ZERLINA

You're sure that nothing else hurts?	E poi non ti duol altro?

MASETTO

Yes, a little	Duolmi un poco
On this foot, and this arm too, and my little finger.	Questo piè, questo braccio e questa mano.

ZERLINA

Well there's not much harm done if the rest's all right.	Via, via: non è gran mal, se il resto è sano.
Come home with your Zerlina;	Vientene meco a casa:
And if you promise	Purchè tu mi prometta
You will never again upset her,	D'essere men geloso,
Then she will find a way to make you better.	Io . . . io ti guarirò, caro il mio sposo.

No. 19. Aria

My dearest lover	[31] Vedrai, carino
Soon shall discover	Se sei buonino,
That sure, sweet remedy	Che bel rimedio
I can prepare.	Ti voglio dar:

For all conditions	È naturale,
Medicine I offer,	Non dà disgusto,
Yet no physicians	E lo speziale
My secret share.	Non lo sa far.
Perfect and rare it is,	È un certo balsamo
Gold cannot buy it;	Che porto addosso:
If you would try it,	Dare tel posso,
Trust to my care.	Se'l vuoi provar.
I bear it with me.	Saper vorresti
Would you know where?	Dove mi sta?

(*She makes him touch her breast.*)

You'll feel it beating now,	Sentilo battere,
Lay your hand there.	Toccami qua.

(*Exeunt.*)

Scene Seven. *The entrance courtyard of Donna Anna's house. It is dark. Leporello, Donna Elvira; then Don Ottavio and Donna Anna with servants and lights. / Recitative*

LEPORELLO
(*still disguising his voice*)

The light of many torches	Di molte faci il lume
Is approaching. My dear, let us remain here	S'avvicina, o mio ben: stiamci qui ascosi,
So that they will not see us.	Finchè da noi si scosta.

DONNA ELVIRA

But, dearest husband,	Ma che temi,
You have no cause to fear them.	Adorato mio sposo?

LEPORELLO

No, of course not.	Nulla, nulla . . .
Simple propriety . . . I'll go and see if they	Certi riguardi . . . Io vo'veder se il lume
Have gone away yet.	È già lontano.

(*aside*)

Oh, how can I	Ah, come
Get rid of this woman?	Da costei liberarmi?

(*to Donna Elvira*)

Wait here for me, beloved . . .	Rimanti, anima bella . . .

(*He makes off.*)

DONNA ELVIRA

Oh, do not leave me!	Ah, non lasciarmi!

No. 20. Sextet

(*aside*)

All alone and in this darkness	[32]	Sola sola, in buio loco,
My heart beats and fear assails me.		Palpitar il cor mio sento;
How I tremble. My courage fails me.		E m'assale un tale spavento,
As if death itself were by.		Che mi sembra di morir.

LEPORELLO
(*feeling his way, aside*)

Curse that doorway? Where's it gone to?	Più che cerco, men ritrovo
Solid darkness all around it!	Questa porta sciagurata . . .
Softly, softly. Now I've found it,	Piano, piano: l'ho trovata,
Off to freedom I can fly.	Ecco il tempo di fuggir.

(*He misses the door. Enter Donna Anna and Don Ottavio in mourning costume, with servants carrying tapers.*)

DON OTTAVIO
(*to Donna Anna*)

No more weeping, my beloved,	Tergi il ciglio, o vita mia!
In my care find consolation.	E da' calma al tuo dolore:
He would not wish this desolation,	L'ombra omai del genitore
Nor that you should grieve in vain.	Pena avrà de' tuoi martir.

DONNA ANNA

Consolation lies in weeping,	Lascia almen alla mia pena
This small comfort I am keeping.	Questo picciolo ristoro.
Only dying, o my beloved,	Sol la morte, o mio tesoro,
Can relieve this bitter pain!	Il mio pianto può finir!

DONNA ELVIRA
(aside, unnoticed)

Ah, where is my dearest husband?	Ah! dov'è lo sposo mio?

LEPORELLO
(aside, from the door, unnoticed)

If she finds me, all is over.	Se mi trovan, son perduto.

DONNA ELVIRA AND LEPORELLO

First the door I must discover,	Una porta là vegg'io
⎰ Then I'll find him once again.	Cheta cheta ⎱ io vo' partir.
⎱ Then I will escape again.	Cheto cheto ⎰

(They try to leave.)

Scene Eight. *Leporello, Donna Elvira, Donna Anna, Don Ottavio, Zerlina, Masetto and servants. Enter Zerlina and Masetto. They meet Donna Elvira and Leporello, who hides his face.*

ZERLINA AND MASETTO

Stop now you scoundrel!	Ferma, briccone!
Where are you going?	Dove ten vai?

DONNA ANNA AND DON OTTAVIO

There is the murderer!	Ecco il fellone!
Why is he here?	Com'era qua?

DONNA ANNA, ZERLINA, DON OTTAVIO AND MASETTO

Death to the criminal,	Ah! mora il perfido,
To the betrayer!	Che m'ha tradito!

DONNA ELVIRA

He is my husband.	È mio marito!
Forgive, forgive!	Pietà, pietà!

DONNA ANNA, ZERLINA, DON OTTAVIO AND MASETTO

It's Donn'Elvira!	È Donn'Elvira,
Loves that deceiver?	Quella ch'io vedo?
I cannot believe her!	Appena il credo ...
No, no! He dies!	No, no: morrà!

(Don Ottavio makes to kill him.)

LEPORELLO
(uncovering his face and falling to his knees before them)

I'm Leporello,	[33]	Perdon, perdono,
Do not believe her.		Signori miei.
That other fellow		Quello io non sono:
Made me deceive her.		Sbaglia, costei;
Oh, let me stay alive,		Viver lasciatemi,
Good people, please!		Per carità!

DONNA ANNA, DONNA ELVIRA, ZERLINA, DON OTTAVIO AND MASETTO

What, Leporello?	Dei, Leporello! ...
Is this delusion?	Che inganno è questo!
	Stupida ⎱
What more confusion	Stupido ⎰ resto:
Can fate devise?	Che mai sarà?

LEPORELLO

Wild and whirling doubts confound me!	Mille torbidi pensieri
Burning, turning, fast and faster.	Mi s'aggiran per la testa:

| To avoid complete disaster | Se mi salvo in tal tempesta, |
| It's a miracle I need. | È un prodigio in verità. |

DONNA ANNA, DONNA ELVIRA, ZERLINA, DON OTTAVIO AND MASETTO

Wild and whirling doubts confound me!	Mille torbidi pensieri
Burning, turning, fast and faster.	Mi s'aggiran per la testa ...
Fresh misfortunes each hour surround us!	Che giornata, o stelle, è questa!
Heaven help us in our need!	Che impensata novità!

(*Exit Donna Anna with servants.*)

Scene Nine. *Leporello, Donna Elvira, Don Ottavio, Zerlina and Masetto. / Recitative*

ZERLINA
(*to Leporello*)

| It was you, then, you brutal creature, | Dunque, quello sei tu che il mio Masetto |
| Who just now so cruelly attacked my poor Masetto! | Poco fa crudelmente maltrattasti! |

DONNA ELVIRA
(*to Leporello*)

| So it was you who deceived me, heartless villain, | Dunque, tu m'ingannasti, o scellerato, |
| By passing yourself off as Don Giovanni! | Spacciandoti con me da Don Giovanni! |

DON OTTAVIO
(*to Leporello*)

| So it was you who came here | Dunque, tu in questi panni |
| In disguise to perpetrate some treachery. | Venisti qui per qualche tradimento! |

ZERLINA

| It is for me to punish him. | A me tocca punirlo. |

DONNA ELVIRA

| No, for me. | Anzi, a me! |

DON OTTAVIO

| No, no, for me. | No, no, a me! |

MASETTO

| Let us all fall upon him at once! | Accoppatelo meco tutti e tre! |

LEPORELLO
*No. 21. Aria**

Oh, have pity please on me. [34]	Ah, pietà, signori miei!
Oh, my lords have pity please on me I pray.	Ah, pietà, pieta di me!
You are quite right, my lord ... and so is she ...	Do ragione a voi ... a lei ...
But I've done nothing wrong today.	Ma il delitto mio non è.

| Don Giovanni by his cunning | Il padron con prepotenza |
| Stole my innocence away. | L'innocenza mi rubò. |

(*to Donna Elvira*)

| Donn'Elvira! Show some mercy! | Donn'Elvira! compatite: |
| How it happened you can say. | Già capite come andò. |

(*to Zerlina*)

| As for who attacked Masetto, I know nothing – | Di Masetto non so nulla. |

(*indicating Donna Elvira*)

Ask this lady if you doubt it,	Vel dirà questa fanciulla:
For we wandered both together	È un oretta *circumcirca*
Round and round an hour or more.	Che con lei girando vò.

(*to Don Ottavio*)

Your lordship wonders	A voi, signore,
Why I should do it?	Non dico niente.
We all make blunders,	Certo timore ...
Don't misconstrue it!	Certo accidente ...

---

* This aria was replaced by a recitative at the 1788 Vienna production.

I saw a light there,	Di fuori chiaro,
And out of fright, Sir ...	Di dentro oscuro ...
Or rather terror ...	Non c'è riparo ...
The darkness ... my error ...	La porta ... il muro ...
Yes ... oh ... dear!	Lo ... il ... la ...
Dodging and hiding ...	Vò da quel lato,
And then colliding ...	Poi, qui celato,
I hope that's clear ...	L'affar si sa ...
All quite clear.	Oh, si sa!
I simply wanted	Ma s'io sapeva
To disappear ...	Fuggia per quà ...

(He escapes.)

Scene Ten. *Donna Elvira, Don Ottavio, Zerlina and Masetto. / Recitative*

DONNA ELVIRA

Stop him! He cheated me! Stop him!	Ferma, perfido, ferma! ...

MASETTO

He's vanished into air!	Il birbo ha l'ali ai piedi ...

ZERLINA

He has tricked us;	Con qual arte
That was clever I must say.	Si sottrasse, l'iniquo!

DON OTTAVIO

I am resolved:	Amici miei,
After all that has happened,	Dopo eccessi si enormi,
We can no longer doubt that Don Giovanni	Dubitar non possiam che Don Giovanni
Was the barbarous murderer	Non sia l'empio uccisore
Of Donna Anna's father. I beg that you will	Del padre di Donn'Anna. In questa casa
All wait here for a short while. I am going	Per poche ore fermatevi: un ricorso
To summon the authorities. Very soon you shall have	Vo' far a chi si deve, e in pochi istanti
The revenge which is due to you.	Vendicarvi prometto.
Our compassion and love, our honour command it.	Così vuole dover, pietade, affetto.

No. 22. Aria*

On your affection relying,	[35]	Il mio tesoro intanto
I leave her to your care.		Andate a consolar,
Ease all her tears and sighing		E del bel ciglio il pianto
And comfort her despair.		Cercate di asciugar.
Tell her I go to serve her,		Ditele che i suoi torti
Tell her I shall avenge her!		A vendicar io vado,
To him who made her suffer,		Che sol di stragi e morti
Justice and death I bear!		Nunzio vogl'io tornar.

(Exeunt.)

Scene Eleven. *Donna Elvira alone.*

DONNA ELVIRA

No. 23. Recitative and Aria

How many evils, O God!	In quali eccessi, o Numi,
Corrupt and wicked beyond imagination,	In quai misfatti orribili, tremendi,
Has this man not committed! Ah no, no longer	È avvolto il sciagurato! Ah, no, non puote
Can Heaven stay its judgment,	Tardar l'ira del cielo ...
Human justice its hand. I seem to hear	La giustizia tardar! Sentir già parmi

---

*For the 1788 Vienna production, *'Il mio tesoro'* was cut – the tenor Morella sang *'Dalla sua pace'* (Act One, scene fourteen) instead. Four new scenes were then inserted after Don Ottavio's recitative. Those for Zerlina and Leporello have never been incorporated into the score (the text and a literal translation are given on page 107). The fourth new scene – Donna Elvira's recitative and aria, written for Catarina Cavalieri – is now traditionally included as Act Two, scene eleven.

The fatal arrow of vengeance	La fatale saetta
Which must strike him and kill him! I see before him	Che gli piomba sul capo! Aperta veggio
The open pit of Hell . . . Wretched Elvira!	Il baratro mortal . . . Misera Elvira,
Still with conflict and sorrow my heart is burning!	Che contrasto d'affetti in sen ti nasce!
Ah why these sighs of pity – this hopeless yearning?	Perchè questi sospiri? e queste ambasce?

Aria

He betrayed the love I gave him.	[36]	Mi tradi, quell'alma ingrata:
Shame and sorrow set me apart.		Infelice, o Dio! mi fa.
He rejects me, yet I would save him,		Ma, tradita e abbandonata,
Still the tears of pity start.		Provo ancor per lui pietà.

Overcome by pain and anger,	Quando sento il mio tormento,
All my blood cries out for vengeance;	Di vendetta il cor favella;
But when I see his mortal danger	Ma, se guardo il suo cimento,
Trembling horror fills my heart.	Palpitando il cor mi va.

(*Exit.*)

Scene Twelve. *A graveyard surrounded by a wall, with various equestrian monuments, including that of the Commendatore. Moonlight. Don Giovanni; then Leporello; the statue of the Commendatore. / Recitative*

DON GIOVANINI
(*He leaps over the wall and enters, laughing.*)

Ha, ha, ha, ha! That was clever.	Ah! ah! ah! ah! questa è buona!
She'll never find me here! A lovely night!	Or lasciala cercar! Che bella notte!
With a moon as bright as daylight: just the night	È più chiara del giorno: sembra fatta
For a hunt – if only I find some prey worth chasing.	Per gir a zonzo a caccia di ragazze.
How late is it?	È tardi?

(*He looks at the clock.*)

I think it's still	Oh, ancor non sono
Two hours short of midnight. I'm longing	Due della notte. Avrei
To know how the business was concluded	Voglia un po' di saper come è finito
Between Leporello and Donn'Elvira.	L'affar tra Leporello e Donn'Elvira:
Was he skilful or clumsy?	S'egli ha avuto giudizio . . .

LEPORELLO
(*off-stage, talking to himself aloud*)

He intended to ruin me on purpose.	Alfin vuole ch'io faccia un precipizio.

DON GIOVANNI

And there he is. Oh, Leporello!	È desso. Oh, Leporello!

LEPORELLO
(*behind the wall*)

Who is that calling?	Chi mi chiama?

DON GIOVANNI

Don't you know your own master?	Non conosci il padron?

LEPORELLO

I only wish I didn't.	Così nol conoscessi!

DON GIOVANNI

What, you scoundrel!	Come? Birbo!

LEPORELLO

Oh, is that you? I'm sorry.	Ah, siete voi. Scusate.

DON GIOVANNI

Well, what happened?	Cosa è stato?

Just now, for your sake, I've been nearly murdered.

Per cagion vostra, io fui quasi accoppato.*

DON GIOVANNI

You took that for an honour, I have no doubt at all.

Ebben, non era questo
Un onore, per te?

LEPORELLO

Please keep such honours!

Signor, vel dono.

DON GIOVANNI

Well, well, come here. I have a nice piece
Of news for you.

Via, via, vien qua: che belle
Cose ti deggio dir!

LEPORELLO

What are you doing here?

Ma cosa fate qui?

DON GIOVANNI

Come in, and I will tell you.

Vien dentro, e lo saprai.

(Leporello climbs over the wall and exchanges his cloak and hat with Don Giovanni.)

I've had a few adventures,
Since you left me in search of other pleasures.
I'll describe them all later; only the best of them
I'll tell you at once.

Diverse istorielle,
Che accadute mi son da che partisti,

Ti dirò un'altra volta; or la più bella
Ti vo' solo narrar.

LEPORELLO

About some woman?

Donnesca, al certo.

DON GIOVANNI

Of course! Young and quite charming,
Lovely face, fetching figure.
We just met in the street there. Well, I approached her,
And took her by the hand. She tried to run away,
So I talked to her gently and she mistook me –
Guess for whom?

C'è dubbio? Una fanciulla
Bella, giovin, galante,
Per la strada incontrai. Le vado appresso,

La prendo per la man: fuggir mi vuole.

Dico poche parole: ella mi piglia

Sai per chi?

LEPORELLO

I don't know.

Non lo so.

DON GIOVANNI

For Leporello.

Per Leporello.

LEPORELLO

For me?

Per me?

DON GIOVANNI

For you!

Per te.

LEPORELLO

Delighted.

Va bene.

DON GIOVANNI

It was she
Who took me by the hand then.

Per la mano
Essa allora mi prende.

LEPORELLO

Better and better.

Ancora meglio.

DON GIOVANNI

She caressed me, embraced me:

M'accarezza, mi abbraccia:

---

* An alternative ten lines of dialogue was written for the 1788 Viennese production.

"Oh, my dear Leporello,
Leporello, my darling ... " And so
I gathered
She was one of your sweethearts.

"Caro il mio Leporello ...
Leporello mio caro ... " Allor
m'accorsi
Ch'era qualche tua bella.

LEPORELLO
(*aside*)

Damn him! Oh, damn him!

Oh, maledetto!

DON GIOVANNI

I took every advantage, until
She recognized me and started screaming.
I heard people and ran off in a hurry, and
quick as lightning,
I climbed that wall and found myself in this
place.

Dell'inganno approfitto. Non so come
Mi riconosce: grida. Sento gente,
A fuggire mi metto, e, pronto pronto,

Per quel muretto in questo loco io monto.

LEPORELLO

And you don't think it odd
To tell me this little story?

E mi dite la cosa
Con tale indifferenza?

DON GIOVANNI

Not at all.

Perchè no?

LEPORELLO

And suppose
I'd been married to the lady?

Ma se fosse
Costei stata mia moglie?

DON GIOVANNI

Even better!

Meglio ancora!

(*He laughs heartily.*)

COMMENDATORE
Dramatic Recitative

This night shall see the end of all your
laughter.

Di rider finirai pria dell'aurora.

Recitative
DON GIOVANNI

Who was speaking?

Chi ha parlato?

LEPORELLO
(*trembling in fear*)

Ah, it must have been
A spirit come from Hell
Who knows you very well.

Ah! qualche anima
Sarà dell'altro mondo,
Che vi conosce a fondo.

DON GIOVANNI

Don't be stupid!
Who goes there? Who goes there?

Taci, sciocco!
Chi va là? chi va là?

(*He draws his sword, and searches here and there through the graveyard, thrusting at some of the statues, etc.*)

COMMENDATORE
Dramatic Recitative

Blasphemer, cold-hearted!
Leave in peace the departed!

Ribaldo audace!
Lascia a' morti la pace.

Recitative
LEPORELLO

There, I told you ...

Ve l'ho detto ...

DON GIOVANNI
(*unmoved and scornful*)

It must be someone out there
In the street trying to mock us.

Sarà qualcun di fuori
Che si burla di noi ...

Look! Is not that the statue
Of the late Commendatore? Just read out
  for me
The inscription.

Ehi! Del Commendatore
Non è questa la statua? Leggi un poco

Quella iscrizion.

LEPORELLO

Excuse me,
I never learnt to read well,
Especially by moonlight . . .

Scusate . . .
Non ho imparato a leggere
A' raggi della luna . . .

DON GIOVANNI

Read, I tell you!

Leggi, dico!

LEPORELLO
(*reading*)

"A profligate traitor did bring me hither,

I await here my vengeance" . . .

"Dell' empio che mi trasse al passo
  estremo
Qui attendo la vendetta" . . .

(*to Don Giovanni*)

You hear that? I'm frightened.

Udiste? . . . Io tremo!

DON GIOVANNI

Ridiculous old fellow!
Tell him to come to supper.
I'll expect him this evening.

O vecchio buffonissimo!
Digli che questa sera
L'attendo a cena meco.

LEPORELLO

Are you mad? Can't you see? Oh, Heavens,
  look, Sir!
How he glares, just as if he were alive!
You'd almost think he heard you
And wanted to reply.

Che pazzia! Ma vi par . . . Oh, Dei! mirate

Che terribili occhiate egli ci dà.
Par vivo! par che senta,
E che voglia parlar . . .

DON GIOVANNI

Do as I say,
Or I will kill you and bury you beside him.

Orsù, va' là,
O qui t'ammazzo e poi ti seppellisco.

LEPORELLO

Gently, gently, my Lord. I will invite him.

Piano, piano, signore: ora ubbidisco.

No. 24. Duet

(*to the statue*)

O statue fair and excellent,
So noble and enlightened . . .

[37] O statua gentilissima
Del gran Commendatore . . .

(*to Don Giovanni*)

My lord, I'm much too frightened,
I don't think this is wise.

Padron, mi trema il core:
Non posso terminar . . .

DON GIOVANNI

Obey me now, or I'll kill you.
I shall not warn you twice.

Finiscila, o nel petto
Ti metto quest'acciar!

LEPORELLO
(*aside*)

He's vicious and capricious.
My blood has turned to ice.

Che impiccio! che capriccio!
Io sentomi gelar.

DON GIOVANNI
(*aside*)

An interesting sensation!
His terror I despise.

Che gusto! che spassetto!
Lo voglio far tremar.

LEPORELLO
(*to the statue*)

O statue fair and excellent,
Your marble will forgive me . . .

O statua gentilissima
Benchè di marmo siate . . .

(to Don Giovanni)

Oh, my lord, were you watching?	Ah, padron mio, mirate
Believe me, I saw him roll his eyes!	Che seguita a guardar.

DON GIOVANNI
(to Leporello)

Die then!	Mori!

LEPORELLO

No, no, wait a moment.	No, no, attendete.

(to the statue)

My master has decided ...	Signor, il padron mio ...
Don't think, dear Sir, that I did ...	Badate ben, non io ...
To invite you home tonight.	Vorria con voi cenar ...

(The statue bows its head)

Ah! ah! ah! I cannot bear it!	Ah! ah! ah! che scena è questa! ...
He bowed his head, I swear it!	Oh, ciel! chinò la testa!

DON GIOVANNI

Oh, stop this silly playing.	Va' là, che se' un buffone ...

LEPORELLO

But look, Sir, believe what I am saying.	Guardate ancor, padrone ...

DON GIOVANNI

What is this wondrous sight?	E che deggio guardar?

LEPORELLO

He, with his head of marble,	Colla marmorea testa
Did nod like this, like this.	Ei fa ... cosi ... cosi ...

(He imitates the statue.)

DON GIOVANNI

He, with his head of marble,	Colla marmorea testa
Did nod like this, like this.	Ei fa cosi ... cosi!

(to the statue)

So answer! If you're able!	Parlate! Se potete,
You'll come to supper?	Verrete a cena?

COMMENDATORE

Yes.	Sì.

LEPORELLO

God save us from temptation!	Mover mi posso appena,
Forgive a wretched sinner.	Mi manca, oh, Dei! la lena!
For Heaven's sake let's run now,	Per carità, partiamo,
Or we shall not survive.	Andiamo via di qua.

DON GIOVANNI

A quite unique occasion!	Bizzarra è inver la scena!
A speaking statue will share my dinner!	Verrà il buon vecchio a cena.
Come, much is to be done now.	A prepararla andiamo,
Our guest will soon arrive.	Partiamo via di qui.

(Exeunt.)

Scene Thirteen. *A room in Donna Anna's house. Donna Anna and Don Ottavio. / Recitative*

DON OTTAVIO

Be calm, my love, I beg you, we soon shall see	Calmatevi, idol mio: di quel ribaldo
This depraved monster punished for his crimes,	Vedrem puniti in breve i gravi eccessi.
And we shall be avenged.	Vendicati sarem.

DONNA ANNA

But my father, my father!	Ma il padre, o Dio! ...

DON OTTAVIO

The grief that Heaven sends us	Convien chinare il ciglio
We must bear as we can. Take comfort, my dearest!	Al volere del ciel. Respira, o cara!
For your bitter bereavement	Di tua perdita amara
I would offer in recompense	Fia domani, se vuoi, dolce compenso
My devotion; you may have tomorrow	Questo cor, questa mano . . .
Both my heart and my hand.	Che il mio tenero amor . . .

DONNA ANNA

Oh, Heavens, how could you!	Oh, Dei! che dite
At a time of such sadness.	In sì tristi momenti . . .

DON OTTAVIO

How long must I still	E che! Vorresti,
Wait the hour of fulfilment?	Con indugi novelli,
Would you increase my sufferings?	Accrescer le mie pene?
How cruel!	Crudele!

DONNA ANNA

No. 25. Recitative and Rondò

I, cruel? Ah, no, beloved!	Crudele? Ah, no, mio bene!
I also suffer	Troppo mi spiace
Too much from these delays. I also long for	Allontanarti un ben che lungamente
That sweet hour of fulfilment. But duty demands it!	La nostr'alma desia . . . Ma il mondo . . . oddio . . .
Do not tempt me in my weakness	Non sedur la mia costanza
To give way, I implore you,	Del sensibil mio core!
For my heart feels as yours, my love speaks for you.	Abbastanza per te mi parla amore.

Rondò

Say no more, my heart's beloved,	[38]	Non mi dir, bell'idol mio,
I am cruel or cold to you;		Che son io crudel con te:
You know well all the love I bear you,		Tu ben sai quant'io t'amai,
You know well that I am true.		Tu conosci la mia fè.
Banish, banish, doubts that wound you,		Calma, calma il tuo tormento,
Or I die of too much sorrow.		Se di duol non vuoi ch'io mora:
Heaven may grant a brighter morrow,		Forse un giorno il cielo ancora
Peace and joy our hearts renew.		Sentirà pietà di me.

(Exit.)

Scene Fourteen. *Don Ottavio alone. / Recitative*

DON OTTAVIO

Yes, I will stand beside her in all her sorrows,	Ah, si segua il suo passo: io vo' con lei
And help her to bear them.	Dividere i martiri.
Heavy burdens grow lighter when we can share them.	Saran meco men gravi i suoi sospiri.

(Exit.)

Scene Fifteen. *A lighted reception room in Don Giovanni's house; a table is laid for a meal. Don Giovanni, Leporello and musicians. / No. 26. Finale*

DON GIOVANNI

Table laid and supper ready.	[39]	Già la mensa è preparata.
(to the musicians)		
While I eat let's have some music.		Voi suonate, amici cari!
I have money and I'll use it,		Giacchè spendo i miei danari,
For the pleasures I prefer.		Io mi voglio divertir.
(He sits down at table.)		
Leporello, must I wait all night?		Leporello, presto in tavola!

LEPORELLO

I am at your service, Sir.	Son prontissimo a servir.

(The servants serve dinner. The musicians begin playing, and Don Giovanni eats.)

That's it! *Cosa rara.*   Bravi! *Cosa rara.*

DON GIOVANNI

Is this music to your liking?   Che ti par del bel concerto?

LEPORELLO

Like my master, it's very rare and   È conforme al vostro merto.
striking.

DON GIOVANNI

And this dish is most delightful.   Ah, che piatto saporito!

LEPORELLO
(aside)

Lord! His appetite is frightful!   Ah, che barbaro appetito!
While he gobbles down great mouthfuls,   Che bocconi da gigante!
I don't even get a share.   Mi par proprio di svenir.

DON GIOVANNI
(aside)

He is watching every mouthful   Nel vedere i miei bocconi
Simply longing for a share.   Gli par proprio di svenir.
                              (to Leporello)
Next course!   Piatto!

LEPORELLO

     Yes, Sir!   Servo.
Now that's Sarti's *Litiganti!*   Evvivano *I litiganti!*

DON GIOVANNI

          Pour the wine now.   Versa il vino!
          (Leporello pours wine into his glass.)
Marzimino, very pleasant!   Eccellente marzimino!

LEPORELLO
(He removes Don Giovanni's dish and serves another, hastily taking some to eat, etc.)

Here's a piece of cold roast pheasant.   Questo pezzo di fagiano
I will eat it quickly, while he's unaware. Piano piano vo' inghiottir.

DON GIOVANNI
(aside)

Stealing my food, greedy peasant!   Sta mangiando, quel marrano:
I'll pretend I do not care.   Fingerò di non capir.

LEPORELLO

That's a tune I have heard once too   Questa poi la conosco pur troppo!
often.

DON GIOVANNI
(calling him without looking at him)

Leporello!   Leporello!

LEPORELLO
(answering with his mouth full)

     Yes, your lordship.   Padron mio.

DON GIOVANNI

Speak more clearly, man, I want some   Parla schietto, mascalzone!
information!

LEPORELLO
(still eating)

I have caught an inflammation;   Non mi lascia una flussione
When I speak it hurts me there.   Le parole proferir.

DON GIOVANNI

How amazing! Can't you whistle?   Mentre io mangio, fischia un poco.

LEPORELLO

I can't blow.   Non so far.

DON GIOVANNI
(looking at him and noticing that he is eating)

Well then . . .   Cos'è?

LEPORELLO

          Forgive me.   Scusate.
You've a cook beyond all praising,   Si eccellente è il vostro cuoco,
I was told and now I know.   Che lo volli anch'io provar.

DON GIOVANNI
(aside)

I've a cook beyond all praising,   Si eccellente è il cuoco mio,
You were told and now you know.   Che lo volle anch'ei provar.

Scene Sixteen. *Don Giovanni, Leporello, musicians, Donna Elvira.*

DONNA ELVIRA
(entering in agitation)

Once more I offer   [40] L'ultima prova
Proof of affection.   Dell'amor mio
For your protection   Ancor vogl'io
You find me here.   Fare con te.

I feel no longer   Più non rammento
Rage and resentment: Gl'inganni tuoi:
Compassion's stronger.   Pietade io sento.

DON GIOVANNI AND LEPORELLO

But why? But why?   Cos'è, cos'è?

(Don Giovanni stands up, and welcomes Donna Elvira with a laugh.)

DONNA ELVIRA
(kneeling)

See, I am kneeling,   Da te non chiede,
But not for my sake   Quest'alma oppressa,
Am I appealing,   Della sua fede
For you, I fear!   Qualche mercè.

DON GIOVANNI

You have surprised me!   Mi meraviglio!
What is my task then?   Cosa volete?
You kneel to ask,   Se non sorgete
So I kneel to hear.   Non resto in piè.

(He kneels before her in an exaggerated manner. After a moment both rise.)

DONNA ELVIRA

Ah, do not mock at me!   Ah, non deridere
I am despairing.   Gli affanni miei!

LEPORELLO
(aside)

There now, just look at me!   Quasi da piangere
Her tears I'm sharing.   Mi fa costei.

DON GIOVANNI

I would not mock at you,   Io ti deridere?
Never, my dear!   Cieli! Perchè?
(still affecting tender solicitude)
What are you asking?   Che vuoi, mio bene?

DONNA ELVIRA

For your repentance.   Che vita cangi.

DON GIOVANNI

Brava!   Brava!

DONNA ELVIRA

Oh cruel heart!   Cor perfido!

DON GIOVANNI

I'll finish supper.	Lascia ch'io mangi.
If you're hungry,	[41] E, se ti piace,
Share it with me.	Mangia con me.

(He goes back to the table, sits down, and carries on eating.)

DONNA ELVIRA

I must abandon you,	Restati, barbaro,
Wallow and fester,	Nel lezzo immondo:
Monstrous example of	Esempio orribile
Iniquity.	D'iniquità.

LEPORELLO
(aside)

If he stays callous	Se non si muove
To her entreaties,	Del suo dolore,
Devoid of feeling	Di sasso ha il core,
He must be.	O cor non ha.

DON GIOVANNI
(drinking etc.)

Women, I drink to you!	Vivan le femmine!
Good wine, I bless you!	Viva il buon vino!
These are the glories of	Sostegno e gloria
Humanity!	D'umanità!

DONNA ELVIRA
(She leaves, then returns with a terrible shriek.)

Ah!   Ah!
(She flees through another door.)

DON GIOVANNI AND LEPORELLO

Whatever was that screaming?   Che grido è questo mai!

DON GIOVANNI
(to Leporello)

Go and see you stupid fellow.   Va' a veder che cosa è stato.

LEPORELLO
(He goes out, and utters an even louder cry before coming back.)

Ah!   Ah!

DON GIOVANNI

Now he's begun to bellow.	Che grido indiavolato!
Leporello, what is there?	Leporello, che cos'è?

LEPORELLO
(entering in terror and closing the door)

Oh, my lord … Let's kneel and pray!	Ah! signor … per carità …
Do not take one step that way!	Non andate fuor di qua …
Made of marble … he advances …	L'uom di.sasso … l'uomo bianco …
Oh, your lordship, I'm losing my senses …	Ah, padrone! io gelo … io manco …
But if you had seen what I have,	Se vedeste … che figura …
Heard the noise those stone feet make!	Se sentiste come fa:

(He imitates the steps of the statue.)

Ta, ta, ta, ta.   Ta, ta, ta, ta.

DON GIOVANNI

I don't understand this nonsense!   Non capisco niente affatto.

LEPORELLO

Ta, ta, ta, ta …   Ta, ta, ta, ta …

You are mad, there's no mistake.	Tu sei matto in verità.

(There is knocking at the door.)

LEPORELLO

There, you hear him?	Ah! sentite!

DON GIOVANNI

Someone's knocking.		Qualcun batte!
Open!	Apri!	

LEPORELLO

I dare not.	Io tremo ...

DON GIOVANNI

Go, I tell you!	Apri, ti doco!

LEPORELLO

Ah!	Ah!

DON GIOVANNI

Open!	Apri!

LEPORELLO

Ah!	Ah!

DON GIOVANNI

Idiot! Whoever stands there knocking	Matto! Per togliermi d'intrico,
Let him dare to come inside.	Ad aprir io stesso andrò.

(He takes the light and goes to open the door.)

LEPORELLO
(aside)

I would rather not receive him;	Non vo' più veder l'amico:
Let me find a place to hide.	Pian pianin m'asconderò.

(He hides under the table.)

Scene Seventeen. *Don Giovanni, Leporello and the statue of the Commendatore; then off-stage chorus. Don Giovanni returns followed by the Commendatore.* [1]

COMMENDATORE

Don Giovanni! You did invite me	Don Giovanni! a cenar teco
To your table. And I accepted.	M'invitasti, e son venuto.

DON GIOVANNI

I can't say you were expected,	Non l'avrei giammai creduto,
But I'll do the best I may.	Ma farò quel che potrò.
	(to Leporello)
Leporello, for our guest here,	Leporello, un'altra cena
Make immediate preparation!	Fa' che subito si porti!

LEPORELLO
(putting his head out from underneath the table)

Oh, my lord! It's the day of our damnation!	Ah, padron! ... Siam tutti morti!

DON GIOVANNI

Quick, obey me!	Vanne, dico ...

(Leporello, obviously terrified, starts to leave.)

COMMENDATORE

Mark what I say!	Ferma un po'!
Earthly food can no longer sustain him	Non si pasce di cibo mortale
Who has tasted of pleasures immortal.	Chi si pasce di cibo celeste:
Not for such things I left Heaven's portal!	Altre cure più gravi di queste,
Greater need brings me hither today.	Altra brama quaggiù mi guidò!

I am shivering as if I'd a fever,   La terzana d'avere mi sembra,
And my muscles are melting away.   E le membra fermar più non so.

DON GIOVANNI

I am listening. Speak out then, and tell me.   Parla, dunque: che chiedi? che vuoi?

COMMENDATORE

Hear with attention, for short is my stay.   Parlo, ascolta: più tempo non ho.

DON GIOVANNI

I am listening, speak out now, I say.   Parla, parla, ascoltando ti sto.

COMMENDATORE

I have fulfilled my promise.   Tu m'invitasti a cena:
Now in return I ask you,   Il tuo dover or sai.
So answer me – will you dine   [2] Rispondimi: verrai
With me, in your turn?   Tu a cenar meco?

LEPORELLO
(from a distance, trembling, to the Commendatore)

        Oh no!   Oibò!
Too busy – please excuse him.   Tempo non ha ... scusate.

DON GIOVANNI

And why should I refuse him?   A torto di viltate
For fear I do not know.   Tacciato mai sarò!

COMMENDATORE

Decide now!   Risolvi!

DON GIOVANNI

      I have decided!   Ho già risolto!

COMMENDATORE

You'll come then?   Verrai?

LEPORELLO
(to Don Giovanni)

     Please tell him no.   Dite di no.

DON GIOVANNI

No man shall call me coward,   Ho fermo il core in petto,
I have resolved: I'll go!   Non ho timor: verrò!

COMMENDATORE

Give me your hand in token!   Dammi la mano in pegno!

DON GIOVANNI

Here it is!   Eccola!
         (He gives a great cry.)
    O God!   Ohimè!

COMMENDATORE

     Afraid?   Cos'hai?

DON GIOVANNI

An icy chill runs through me.   Che gelo è questo mai!

COMMENDATORE

Penitence still can save you   Pentiti, cangia vita:
Or face the final sentence.   È l'ultimo momento!

DON GIOVANNI
(trying in vain to get free)

No, I despise repentance.   No, no, ch'io non mi pento:
Off with you! Leave my sight!   Vanne lontan da me!

	COMMENDATORE	
Profligate, brutal, vicious!		Pentiti, scellerato!

DON GIOVANNI

Vain, old and repetitious.	No, vecchio infatuato!

COMMENDATORE

Penitence!	Pentiti.

DON GIOVANNI

No!	No.

COMMENDATORE AND LEPORELLO

Yes.	Si.

DON GIOVANNI

No.	No.

COMMENDATORE

Now dawns your endless night!	Ah! tempo più non v'è!

(Fire and earthquake all around. The Commendatore disappears.)

DON GIOVANNI

Limbs all aflame yet shivering . . .	Da qual tremore insolito . . .
Heart pierced with unknown agony . . .	Sento assalir gli spiriti . . .
Round me a void is quivering . . .	Donde escono quei vortici
Can this be Hell indeed?	Di fuoco pien d'orror! . . .

INVISIBLE CHORUS

Take the reward of evil.	Tutto a tue colpe è poco.
Worse yet remains in store!	Vieni: c'è un mal peggior!

DON GIOVANNI

Who rends my soul with suffering?	Chi l'anima mi lacera! . . .
Who turns my blood to bitterness?	Chi m'agita le viscere! . . .
Must madness, pain, and terror	Che strazio! ohimè! che smania!
Possess me evermore?	Che inferno! . . . che terror! . . .

LEPORELLO

He writhes in desperation,	Che ceffo disperato! . . .
In torments of damnation!	Che gesti da dannato! . . .
His cries and groans appal me!	Che gridi! che lamenti! . . .
I can endure no more!	Come mi fa terror! . . .

INVISIBLE CHORUS

Take the reward of evil.	Tutto a tue colpe è poco.
Worse yet remains in store!	Vieni: c'è un mal peggior!

(The flames increase. Don Giovanni sinks into them.)*

DON GIOVANNI

Ah!	Ah!

LEPORELLO

Ah!	Ah!

Scene Eighteen. *Leporello, Donna Elvira, Donna Anna, Don Ottavio, Zerlina and Masetto.*

DONNA ELVIRA, ZERLINA, DON OTTAVIO AND MASETTO
(entering with Donna Anna and officers of the law)

Where is the evil one?	[42]	Ah! dove è il perfido,
He who betrayed us		Dove è l'indegno?
Shall not evade us:		Tutto il mio sdegno
Vengeance we owe.		Sfogar io vo'.

---

* The final scene was omitted in the 1788 Vienna production, and the other characters entered, at the very moment Don Giovanni was engulfed by hell-fire, to witness his fate in silence.

DONNA ANNA

When we have found him,	Solo mirandolo
Seized him and bound him,	Stretto in catene,
Then shall my sorrow	Alle mie pene
Some respite know.	Calma darò.

LEPORELLO

Don't hope to find him,	Più non sperate
You're far behind him,	Di ritrovarlo ...
He's gone much further	Più non cercate:
Than you should go.	Lontano andò.

DONNA ANNA, DONNA ELVIRA, ZERLINA, DON OTTAVIO AND MASETTO

What are you saying?	Cos'è? Favella!

LEPORELLO

This great big statue ...	Venne un colosso ...

DONNA ANNA, DONNA ELVIRA, ZERLINA, DON OTTAVIO AND MASETTO

Quickly, explain yourself!	Via, presto, sbrigati!

LEPORELLO

I'm trying to tell you ...	Ma, se non posso ...

DONNA ANNA, DONNA ELVIRA, ZERLINA, DON OTTAVIO AND MASETTO

What are you saying? Quickly now!	Presto! Favella! Sbrigati!

LEPORELLO

When we had supped, he ...	Tra fumo e fuoco ...
Don't interrupt me ...	Badate un poco ...
Stony and smoking ...	L'uomo di sasso ...
We were both choking ...	Fermate il passo ...
Burst through the door there ...	Giusto là sotto
Stamped on the floor there ...	Diede il gran botto,
Up came the devil and	Giusto là il diavolo
Dragged him below.	Se 'l trangugiò.

DONNA ANNA, DONNA ELVIRA, ZERLINA, DON OTTAVIO AND MASETTO

Strange revelation!	Stelle! Che sento!

LEPORELLO

No exaggeration!	Vero è l'evento.

DONNA ELVIRA

I saw the spectre	Ah, certo è l'ombra
Who brought him low.	Che m'incontrò.

DONNA ANNA, ZERLINA, DON OTTAVIO AND MASETTO

She saw the spectre	Ah, certo è l'ombra
Who brought him low.	Che l'incontrò.

DON OTTAVIO

So the vengeance for which we pleaded,	Or che tutti, o mio tesoro,
O my dear one, Heaven has granted.	Vendicati siam dal cielo,
Now the vows which his crimes impeded	Porgi, porgi a me un ristoro:
May our hearts and hands fulfil!	Non mi far languire ancor.

DONNA ANNA

Love, I beg you, for one year longer	Lascia, o caro, un anno ancora
Let me mourn my father still.	Allo sfogo del mio cor.
No commandment could be stronger	Al desio di chi t'adora
Than a faithful lover's will.	Ceder deve un fido amor.

DON OTTAVIO

No commandment could be stronger	Al desio di chi m'adora
Your desire shall be my will.	Ceder deve un fido amor.

DONNA ELVIRA

I shall end my days in fasting,	Io men vado in un ritiro
Praying for that wicked sinner!	A finir la vita mia!

ZERLINA AND MASETTO

We will get our friends together,	Noi, { Masetto, Zerlina, a casa andiamo,
And enjoy a splendid dinner!	A cenar in compagnia.

LEPORELLO

I must find a better master –	Ed io vado all'osteria
Serving is my only skill.	A trovar padron miglior.

ZERLINA, MASETTO AND LEPORELLO

While that evil man can go	Resti dunque quel birbon
To his home in Hell below!	Con Proserpina e Pluton.
So good people, pay attention:	E noi tutti, o buona gente,
In accordance with convention,	Ripetiam allegramente
We the moral now will show.	L'antichissima canzon.

DONNA ANNA AND DONNA ELVIRA

Sinners end as they begin!	Questo è il fin di chi fa mal!

DONNA ANNA, DONNA ELVIRA, DON OTTAVIO, MASETTO AND LEPORELLO

Sinners end!	Questo è il fin!

ZERLINA

Sinners end as they begin!	Questo è il fin di chi fa mal!

DONNA ANNA, DONNA ELVIRA, ZERLINA, DON OTTAVIO, MASETTO AND LEPORELLO

Sinners end as they begin.	Questo è il fin di chi fa mal:
All who scorn the life eternal	E de' perfidi la morte
Their eternal death shall win!	Alla vita è sempre ugual!

Finis.

Stanley Clarkson as the Commendatore, Frederick Sharp as Don Giovanni and Edmund Donlevy as Leporello in the 1949 Sadler's Wells production by Geoffrey Dunn designed by Tanya Moiseiwitsch (photo Angus McBean © Harvard Theatre Collection)

Additional Scenes

These three scenes were added between the tenth and the eleventh scenes of the second act by Mozart and da Ponte for the 1788 production in Vienna. Since then they have rarely been performed, and this literal translation is not part of the rest of the translation.

(Act Two) Scene Eleven. *Zerlina and Leporello. / Recitative.*

ZERLINA
(With a knife in her hand, and leading Leporello out by the hair.)

You stay there!	Rèstati qua!

LEPORELLO

For pity's sake, Zerlina!	Per carità, Zerlina!

ZERLINA

Eh, there's no pity for the likes of you.	Eh, non c'è carità pei pari tuoi.

LEPORELLO

So, you want to cut out ...	Dunque, cavar mi vuoi? ...

ZERLINA

Your hair, your head, your heart and your eyes!	I capelli, la testa, il core e gli occhi!

LEPORELLO

Listen, my little dear ...	Senti, carina mia ...

(He tries to make eyes at her, but Zerlina pushes him away with a threat.)

ZERLINA

Watch out if you touch me!	Guai se mi tocchi!
You'll see, you scum of a rogue,	Vedrai, schiuma de' birbi,
What you get for doing wrong to girls.	Qual premio n'ha chi le ragazze ingiuria.

LEPORELLO
(aside)

Deliver me, o Gods, from this fury!	Liberatemi, o Dei, da questa fùria!

(Zerlina drags Leporello behind her throughout the scene. Enter a peasant.)

Masetto, olà, Masetto!	Masetto, olà, Masetto!
Where the devil has he gone? ... Servants, people!	Dove diavolo è ito? ... servi, gente!
No-one comes ... no-one hears.	Nessun vien ... nessun sente.

LEPORELLO

Be careful, for pity's sake: don't drag me As though I were tied to a horse's tail!	Fa' piano, per pietà: non strascinarmi A coda di cavallo!

ZERLINA

You'll see, you'll see how the party ends!	Vedrai, vedrai come finisce il ballo!
Quickly, over here with that chair!	Presto, qua quella sedia!

LEPORELLO

There it is!	Eccola!

ZERLINA

Sit down!	Siedi!

LEPORELLO

I'm not tired.	Stanco non son.

ZERLINA

Sit down, or with these hands	Siedi, o con queste mani
I'll tear out your heart and throw it to the dogs.	Ti strappo il cor e poi lo getto ai cani.

LEPORELLO
(sitting down)

I'll sit. But, please,	Siedo. Ma tu, di grazia,
Put down that razor:	Metti giù quel rasoio:
Perhaps you would care to shave me?	Mi vuoi forse sbarbar?

ZERLINA

Yes, you rascal:	Sì, mascalzone:
I'll give you a close shave.	Io sbarbare ti vo' senza sapone.

LEPORELLO

Ye Gods above!	Eterni Dei!

ZERLINA

Give me your hand!	Dammi la man!

LEPORELLO
(hesitating)

My hand?	La mano?

ZERLINA
(menacingly)

The other one!	L'altra!

LEPORELLO

But what d'you want to do to me?	Ma che vuoi farmi?

ZERLINA

I'll do . . . I'll do what I please.	Voglio far . . . voglio far quello che parmi!

(Zerlina ties Leporello's hands with a kerchief. The peasant helps her.)

Duet

LEPORELLO

By these two little hands,	Per queste tue manine
White and very soft,	Candide e tenerelle,
By that fresh complexion	Per questa fresca pelle,
Have pity on me!	Abbia pietà di me!

ZERLINA

There's no pity for you, rogue,	Non v'è pietà, briccone:
I am a furious tigress,	Son una tigre irata,
An asp, a lioness!	Un aspide, un leone!
No, no, no pity for you!	No, no, pietà non v'è!

LEPORELLO

Ah! If it were possible to escape . . .	Ah! di fuggir si provi . . .

ZERLINA

You're dead, if you move.	Sei morto, se ti muovi.

LEPORELLO

Barbarous, unjust Gods!	Barbari, ingiusti Dei!
Who allowed me to fall	In mano di costei
Into such hands?	Che capitar mi fe'?

ZERLINA

Barbarous betrayer!	Barbaro traditore!
If only I had your master's heart	Del tuo padrone il core
Here, with yours.	Avessi qui con te.

(She ties him to the chair and ties the cord to the window.)

LEPORELLO

Ah! Don't squeeze me so tightly:	Deh! non mi stringer tanto:
My breath is leaving me.	L'anima mia sen va.

Whether it comes or goes,	Sen vada o resti: intanto
You won't be leaving here!	Non partirai di qua!

LEPORELLO

What squeezes, o Gods, what blows!	Che strette, o Dei, che bòtte!
Is it day, or is it night?	E giorno, ovvero è notte?
What earthquake tremors!	Che scosse di tremuoto!
What inky darkness!	Che buia oscurità!

ZERLINA

What joy and with delight,	Di gioia e di diletto
I feel my heart sparkle.	Sento brillarmi il petto.
This is the way	Così, così, cogli uomini,
That men should be dealt with.	Così, così si fa.

Scene Twelve. *Leporello and a peasant.*

LEPORELLO

Recitative

Friend, for pity's sake,	Amico, per pietà,
A little cold water or I die!	Un poco d'acqua fresca o ch'io mi moro!

(*Exit peasant.*)

Just look how tightly	Guarda un po' come stretto
The murderess has tied me! If I could only	Mi legò l'assassina! Se potessi
Free myself with my teeth . . . Oh, may the devil	Liberarmi coi denti . . . Oh, venga il diavolo
Come to untie these knots!	A disfar questi gruppi!
I'd like to see this rope broken . . .	Io vo' vedere di rompere la corda . . .
How strong it is! I'm afraid of death!	Come è forte! Paura della morte!
And you, Mercury, protector of thieves,	E tu, Mercurio, protettor de' ladri,
Protect a gentleman! Courage . . .	Proteggi un galantuom'! Coraggio . . .

(*He gives a sharp tug, and the window to which the end of the rope is tied collapses. Leporello runs off dragging the window-frame and chair behind him.*)

Bravo!	Bravo!
Before that woman comes back,	Pria che costei ritorni,
I'll have to put wings on my heels,	Bisogna dar di sprone alle calcagna,
And drag a mountain behind me, if I must.	E strascinar, se occorre, una montagna.

Scene Thirteen. *Zerlina, Donna Elvira; then Masetto with two peasants.*

ZERLINA

Come, come, my lady!	Andiam, andiam, signora!
See how I have	Vedrete in qual maniera
Fixed the rascal.	Ho concio il scellerato.

DONNA ELVIRA

Ah, let me vent	Ah, sopra lui
My rage on him!	Si sfoghi il mio furore!

ZERLINA

Heavens! How	Stelle! In qual modo
Has the rascal saved his skin?	Si salvò quel briccone?

ELVIRA

His wicked master must have released him.	L'avrà sottratto l'empio suo padrone.

ZERLINA

It was him and no mistake: I'll tell	Fu desso senza fallo. Anche di questo
Don Ottavio about this as well; he is supposed	Informiam Don Ottavio: a lui si aspetta
To act for all of us, or to demand vengeance.	Far per noi tutti, o domandar vendetta.

(*Exit.*)

Discography *by David Nice*

In addition to a highlights CD of the Klemperer set (not currently available complete), historic performances of scenes and arias can be heard on a six-LP set, 'Les introuvables du chant Mozartien', from EMI Pathe-Marconi. Arnold Östman's authentic-instruments Drottningholm performance, with a cast including Håken Hagegård, Della Jones and Arleen Auger, will be available on Decca later this year.

	Busch	Furtwängler	J. Krips	Giulini
Conductor	Busch	Furtwängler	J. Krips	Giulini
Company/Orchestra	**Glyndebourne Festival Opera**	**Vienna State Opera**	**Vienna State Opera**	**Philharmonia Orch & Chorus**
Date	*1936*	*1954*	*1958*	*1959*
Don Giovanni	J. Brownlee	C. Siepi	C. Siepi	E. Wächter
Donna Anna	I. Souez	E. Grümmer	S. Danco	J. Sutherland
Donna Elvira	L. Helletsgruber	E. Schwarzkopf	L. Della Casa	E. Schwarzkopf
Don Ottavio	K. von Pataky	A. Dermota	A. Dermota	L. Alva
Leporello	S. Baccaloni	O. Edelmann	F. Corena	G. Taddei
Commendatore	D. Franklin	D. Ernster	K. Böhme	G. Frick
Zerlina	A. Mildmay	E. Berger	H. Gueden	G. Sciutti
Masetto	R. Henderson	W. Berry	W. Berry	P. Cappuccilli
UK LP number	—	(EMI) EX 290667-3 (3)	—	—
UK tape number	—	(EMI) EX 290667-5 (3)	—	—
UK CD number	(EMI) CHS7 61030-2 (3)	—	(Decca) 411 626-2DM3 (3)	(EMI) CDS7 472608 (3)
US LP number	—	(Angel) EX 290667-3 (3)	—	—
US tape number	—	(Angel) EX 290667-5 (3)	—	—
US CD number	(Angel) CHS7 61030-2 (3)	—	(London) 411 626-2LM3 (3)	(Angel) CDS7 472608 (3)

Conductor Company/ Orchestra Date	C. Davis Royal Opera 1973	Maazel Paris Opera 1979	Haitink Glyndebourne Festival Ch, LPO 1984	Kubelik Bavarian Radio 1986	Karajan Deutsche Oper Ch, BPO 1986
Don Giovanni	I. Wixell	R. Raimondi	T. Allen	A. Titus	S. Ramey
Donna Anna	M. Arroyo	E. Moser	C. Vaness	J. Varady	A. Tomowa-Sintow
Donna Elvira	K. Te Kanawa	K. Te Kanawa	M. Ewing	A. Auger	A. Baltsa
Don Ottavio	S. Burrows	K. Riegel	K. Lewis	T. Moser	G. Winbergh
Leporello	W. Ganzarolli	J. Van Dam	R. Van Allen	R. Panerai	F. Furlanetto
Commendatore	L. Roni	J. Macurdy	D. Kavrakos	J.-H. Rootering	P. Burchuladze
Zerlina	M. Freni	T. Berganza	E. Gale	E. Mathis	K. Battle
Masetto	R. Van Allan	M. King	J. Rawnsley	R. Scholze	A. Malta
UK LP number	—	—	—	(Eurodisc) 302 435 (3)	(DG) 419 179-1GH3 (3)
UK tape number	—	—	—	—	(DG) 419 179-4GH3 (3)
UK CD number	(Philips) 416 406-2PH3 (3)	(CBS) M3K 35192 (3)	(EMI) CDS7 47037-8 (3)	(Eurodisc) 353 263 (3)	(DG) 419 179-2GH3 (3)
US LP number	—	—	—	—	(DG) 419 179-1GH3 (3)
US tape number	—	—	—	—	(DG) 419 179-4GH3 (3)
US CD number	(Philips) 416 406-2PH3 (3)	(CBS) M3K 35192 (3)	(Angel) CDS7 47037-8 (3)	—	(DG) 419 179-2GH3 (3)

Bibliography

Alfred Einstein's *Mozart, his Character, his Work* (London, 1969), which has an illuminating passage on the opera in the context of Mozart's whole output, contains a surprising quantity of detailed observation for so short and readable a text. *Three Mozart Operas* by R.B. Moberly (London, 1967), *The Operas of Mozart* by William Mann (London, 1977), Hermann Abert's *Mozart's Don Giovanni* (extracted from Jahn's biography of *Mozart*, which Abert revised for the 6th edition, and translated by P. Gellhorn) (London, 1976) and Julian Rushton's *Cambridge Opera Handbook* on the opera (C.U.P., 1981) each study the opera in depth. Yet E.J. Dent's *Mozart's Operas, A Critical Study* (London, 1913, 1947), the first major study of them in English, still makes an excellent introduction combining as it does scholarship and wit.

The controversial studies of Joseph Kerman (*Opera as Drama*, revised ed. Faber, 1989), Brigid Brophy (*Mozart, the Dramatist*, revised ed. Libris, 1988) and Fritz Noske (*The Signifier and the Signified*, The Hague, 1977) may be recommended for further reading.

More recent publications of distinction include Andrew Steptoe's clearly argued book about *The Mozart-Da Ponte Operas* (Oxford, 1988), which includes a refreshing approach to commonly held assumptions and acknowledges the vital part of the librettist in the collaborative process of opera composition. H.C. Robbins Landon has contributed two beautifully illustrated books about Mozart (*1791: Mozart's Last Year*, 1988, and *Mozart, The Golden Years 1781-1791*, 1989, both published by Thames and Hudson), in which his elegant and extremely well-researched text is dotted with contemporary quotations. Eduard Mörike's delightful *Mozart's Journey to Prague* (trans. Loewenstein-Wertheim, Calder, 1985) remains a favourite treat for lovers of this opera in particular, since it concerns an incident which might have occurred on Mozart's way to the first performance.

Emily Anderson's translation of *The Letters of Mozart and his Family* (3 vols, London, 1938) vividly fills in the background to the composition.

The only English biography of da Ponte is by April FitzLyon *Lorenzo da Ponte* (London, 1982). His *Memorie*, translated by Elisabeth Abbott (Philadelphia, 1929) make fascinating reading. The passage in Patrick J. Smith's *The Tenth Muse: A Historical Study of the Opera Libretto* (London, 1971) is the best survey of contemporary librettos.

The Making of an Opera by John Higgins (Secker & Warburg, 1978) follows the preparation of Peter Hall's 1978 Glyndebourne production.

Contributors

Michael F. Robinson, Senior Lecturer in Music at University College, Cardiff, is the author of *Opera Before Mozart*.

David Wyn Jones is Lecturer in Music at University College, Cardiff, and is the co-editor of the Haydn Yearbook.

Christopher Raeburn, Manager of Classical Recordings for Decca, has researched extensively into performances of 18th-century music, especially the operas of Mozart.